TABLE OF CONTENTS

PREFACE

A decade ago some wanted me to use the word 'ethos', however, I did not want to use a word in the Writ of Certiorari that a judge might misinterpret since the word ethos uses 'or', although, that word is reserved for use in oral arguments if the United States Supreme Court grants the writ of certiorari, or in a future published book if the writ of certiorari is denied. The moral nature must accompany the distinguishing character, sentiments, and guiding beliefs of a person, group, or institution, therefore, the debauchers, adulterers, smearers, and slanderers - especially under oath that disregards the guiding beliefs of an institution and community of interests - cannot use the word ethos, especially when they do not also have a distinguishing character and sentiments directly involved, therefore the opposition cannot apply for the word ethos nor refute my usage of the word ethos.

UNITED STATES DISTRICT COURT, WESTERN DISTRICT OF NORTH CAROLINA STATESVILLE DIVISION

David Thomas Silvers Sr. Plaintiff	CIVIL RIGHTS AMENDED COMPLAINT
vs.	(42 U.S.C. §1983, §1985)
Iredell County Department of Social Services, D.S.S. Dir. Donald Wall, in individual and official capacities; Asst. D.A. Paxton Butler, in individual and official capacities; City of Statesville, N.C. Defendant(s)	CIVIL NO. 5:15CV83-RLV

Here comes David Thomas Silvers Sr. pro se redressing grievances and brings this civil action under 42 U.S.C §1983 and §1985 for acts committed by defendant(s) under color of state law which deprived plaintiff of security, privacy, liberty, and property without due process of law in violation of the First, Fourth, Fifth, and Fourteenth Amendments of the United States Constitution, and International Human Rights.

1. On December 26th 2000, after plaintiff as father sired two girls, then two boys, with custody of his eldest through a personal, private, and mutual agreement with the first mother, father was awarded custody by the Chief Judge in Circuit Court of Baltimore County, Maryland against second mother for youngest three sired.

2. On April 21st 2003, the father, after presiding with prudent trust, security, and efficiency while providing significant benefits for his sired gender balance and merited functional family on deeded private property of 333 North Greenbriar Road. Statesville, N.C., won the Appeal of custody in Silvers v. Silvers heard by the Maryland Supreme Court upholding the Circuit Court in favor of the father.

3. On June 5th 2004, after youngest three sired had already promised and wanted to return in their father's custody, they visited their mother over the

summer, and then with reckless indifference of the father's First, Fourth, and Fourteenth Amendments of the U.S. Constitution while depriving privacy "relating to marriage procreation, contraception, family relationships, and child rearing and education", Paul v. Davis, 424 U.S. 693 (1976), and International Human Rights that prevents "interfering with his privacy, family, home or correspondence, nor attacks upon his honor and reputation", Iredell County D.S.S. in Statesville N.C. under Donald Wall with supervisory liability, Monell v. Department of Soc. Serv. 436 U.S. 658 (1978), recklessly, belatedly, and profanely pandered while prejudiced for the mother whom during the prior four years contested custody every year with no credibility from any Court in the State she resided, and was again contesting custody with no significant benefits while coercing,

and afflicting oppression on father's sired children
after father had done everything he could to
secure the stable health, happiness, and success
for his sired children, then an Ad Litem was
appointed and father's sired children were placed
in foster care while father had supervised
visitations in the socialistic D.S.S. building, and the
mother had unsupervised visitations whereas the
mother continued coercing while father's freedom
of speech was suppressed by social workers
referring to supervision from Donald Wall that was
in the building during visitations, then D.S.S.
conspired with Assistant District Attorney of Iredell
County, Paxton Butler, and upon information from
father's counsel that Paxton Butler coerced with a
threat of charges to obstruct justice if father
proceeded with custody hearing there was slander
from hearsay on a family Court stand by a social

worker, and then custody was prejudicially and illegitimately taken by Iredell County and the City of Statesville, then given to the mother advocating unmerited dysfunctional fatherless families degenerating population with no merit nor ethics nor justice.

4. On or about the first week of March 2005, father expressed non-threatening freedom of speech in a religious writing to the Ad Litem regarding honorable achievements in his sired family that were disregarded from others salaciously and treacherously coercing father's sired children into a breach of promise, and disrespectful and ungrateful slander, then Ad Litem conspired with Paxton Butler whom interfered with correspondence, then circulated without consent causing substantial burdens for the father as an independent moderate exercising the First

Amendment "as he believes to be acceptable to him" - James Madison, to respond without recompense to a mob of popular public opinion that continuously vacillates to liberal left or religious right with reckless indifference of First, Fourth, and Fourteenth Amendments of the U.S. Constitution, and International Human Rights while disregarding sacred honor, sincere providence, pledge, civilization, and dignity, then prejudicially with discrimination and excessive entanglement with the free of exercise of religion on private property, and without significant benefits, and without a legitimate and neutral government interest, coerce into bad faith by advocating alienating, degenerating, and adultery or debauching from extraneous encroachment, genocidal persecution, profane pandering, stereotypical stigmatization, and totalitarian oppression of the stability, health, happiness, and honorable achievements of the father, and his sired children.

5. On March 11th 2005, Paxton Butler with negligence and without significant benefits used what he wanted from the correspondence between father and Ad Litem while disregarding the exculpatory claim in the correspondence stating there was libelous slander from plaintiff's sired children coerced by their mother, then for personal political gain and malfeasance with reckless indifference of father's First, Fourth, and Fourteenth Amendments of the U.S. Constitution, and International Human Rights, prejudicially and corruptly caused substantial harm and substantial burdens with attacks on father's honor and reputation by maliciously, insensibly and needlessly filing spurious and totalitarian charges

of "indecent liberties", and "statutory rape", then on a later date used libelous slander for an abuse of process with improper purpose of misleading with reckless intent to deceive a Grand Jury by misrepresenting evidence with omission of significant information that would negate probable cause such as father's claims that the mother with no credibility coerced father's sired children into slandering their father when there was sanctity, virginity, fertility, stable health, happiness, honorable achievements, and promise from plaintiff's adolescent daughter which was better than coercing into unstable hatred and flunking from oppression that Paxton Butler advocated while the father absolutely claims separation of Church and State after the father provided significant benefits for his sired children, and with neutral interest of respecting the City, however the

City has no neutral interest of respecting the father, and his sired children on private property nor respecting the free exercise of religion and private Church separation that prevents totalitarian oppression by the State.

6. On or about September 19th 2007, after 2 ½ years without due process, and more invasions of privacy with the reckless indifference of the father's Fifth and Fourteenth Amendments of the U.S. Constitution resulting in the father's indignation, the father protested the following misconduct by Paxton Butler:

   a. Interfered with custody hearing by coercing obstruction of justice.

   b. Interfered with privacy.

   c. Interfered with sired gender balance and merited functional family.

   d. Interfered with home.

e. Interfered with correspondence protesting with a, b, c, and d.

f. Attacks upon honor and reputation that damaged wages and benefits that diminished earning capacity from prejudiced charges without due process.

The foregoing resulted in a similar expression to Sodom and Gomorrah of Genesis Chapter 19 in the sacred Bible in every Court, then on October 12th 2007, there was more carelessness and negligence by Paxton Butler after harassingly, maliciously, and incompetently deprived property by charging the father with "fraudulently burning dwelling" when higher State Courts previously held that charge does not apply when no substantial harm to another's property nor fraudulently collecting insurance.

7. On January 25th 2009, after already appearing in Iredell County Superior Court for four years without due process, the father was incarcerated until a dismissal and release on August 28th 2012. During the aforementioned time the father was deprived of liberty and due process from abuse of process by improperly sending father back and forth a few times to a State mental institution forcing harmful drugs after manufacture previously settled a class action, and when the father had already been cleared by the same State mental institution in October 2007.

8. As a result of the defendant(s) misconduct, the plaintiff sustained substantive personal injuries that include, but not limited to, the following: irreparably damaging past, present, and future wages and benefits, diminished earning capacity, pain and suffering from mental anguish and

emotional distress from conscience shocking and antagonism with attempts of humiliation, indignities and embarrassment with damages to honor and reputation, and restrictions from the trammeling of personal freedom, including, but not limited to, physical activity, education, personal fulfillment, parental responsibilities, family relations, friend relations, access to media and technology, travel, enjoyment, and expression.

9. On November 25th 2014, expunction was granted by Sr. Resident Superior Court Judge of Iredell County for the "indecent liberties" and "statutory rape" charges.

10. This filing serves as plaintiff's fatherly responsibility while supporting the higher Courts against invasions of privacy and harassment by mob rule using tyranny of the majority and totalitarian State to subjugate while negligent of

census gender imbalance and legitimate trade, then degenerate and debauch a sired gender balance and merited functional family. After the uncivilized majority cannot comprehend the plaintiff's code with https://github.com/dtsilvers, the majority might not comprehend herein, since the majority already did not comprehend the betterment of the father's sired children prior to excessive entanglement after "Democracy comes into being, after the poor have conquered their opponents, slaughtering some and banishing the rest" - Plato, when the father was willing to let his daughter, whom promised then was treacherously coerced into slander, leave if she had wanted to leave, and save his sons, whom were brainwashed by sleazy trash into slander, after questioning whether respectfully asking her father for his daughter's hand in marriage, or coercing and forcefully taking for pimping by mob rule that can be prevented with property, separation of Church and State, and the right to privacy. After a father that sired his children and provided significant benefits, a father does not want a spurious imposter from mob rule whom was not present nor providing any significant benefits to conjecture on what happened in a father's private home after his sired children were healthily stable, happy, and successful while not harming others that are substantially harming his children and their father from a totalitarian State recklessly negligent of U.S. Constitutional Amendments, and International Human Rights written as a result of atrocities by mob rule from tyranny of the majority and totalitarianism of the WWII German Democracy, when father's sired family were better than the perversions of mob rule that peep, pander, and pimp into a father's home. The seriousness of the redress of grievances is related when considering that after father expressed his First Amendment from the free exercise of religion, then protesting with freedom of speech in writing, and then after Paxton Butler voided the First Amendment, the foregoing could have resulted in the father exercising his Second Amendment, and that was inferred by a Judge in family Court in March 2005 that warned the mother to get an escort while out of the home from the potential retribution of indignation from the father after the mother had coerced his sired children into ungrateful slander and then attempted to subjugate their father using a spurious imposter of mob rule while the family Court Judge knows the record shows that fathers have exercised their

Second Amendment after less damage and indignation that the plaintiff experienced.

PRAYER FOR RELIEF

1. Plaintiff seeks compensatory damages in the amount of $6,760,000, calculated from $260K per year job offer in April 2013 as a software engineer that was only contingent on criminal history while amount is retroactive from time of 2005 charges until age of retirement from irreparably damaging past, present, and future wages and benefits while diminishing earning capacity.

2. Plaintiff seeks punitive damages in the amount of $6,760,000, for pain and suffering with mental anguish, emotional distress, and restrictions on personal freedom from 7 ½ years without due process while 3 ½ years

were wrongfully incarcerated with unnecessary mental evaluations and forcing harmful drugs.

3. Such other and further relief as the Court may deem just and proper.

DECLARATION UNDER PENALTY OF PERJURY

The undersigned declares under penalty that he is the plaintiff in the above action, and that plaintiff read above complaint, and information contained therein is true and correct. 28 U.S.C. §1746; 18 U.S.C. §1621.

This the _____ day of _____ 2015

BY: _____

David Thomas Silvers Sr.

UNITED STATES DISTRICT COURT, WESTERN DISTRICT OF NORTH CAROLINA STATESVILLE DIVISION

<u>David Thomas Silvers Sr.</u> <u>[pro se]</u> Plaintiff vs. Iredell County Department of Social Services, D.S.S. Dir. Donald Wall, in individual and official capacities; Asst. D.A. Paxton Butler, in individual and <u>official capacities; City</u> <u>of Statesville, N.C.</u> Defendant(s)	CIVIL NO. 5:15CV83-RLV

MOTION FOR DEFAULT JUDGMENT

NOW COMES plaintiff David Thomas Silvers Sr. pro se and requests the Court, pursuant to Rule 55 (b) (1) of the Federal Rules of Civil Procedure, for the entry of a judgment by default against the defendant, Paxton Butler, in individual, and official capacities for the City of Statesville, N.C. The plaintiff has demonstrated due diligence in conformity with Federal Rules of Civil Procedure while a few of the claims in the Amended Complaint was that the defendant, Paxton Butler, in individual, and official capacities for the City of Statesville, N.C., obstructed justice, abused process, and deprived due process. After plaintiff already stated in the complaint that there was disregard for process and procedure, then when similar disregard is repeated through Federal Rules of Civil Procedure, then Paxton Butler and the City of Statesville, N.C. do not deserve further consideration when "mob-rule is a rough sea for the ship of state to ride, every wind of oratory stirs up the waters and deflects the course" - Plato, such as not only the honorable achievements in plaintiff's sired gender balance and merited functional family, and due process, now Federal Rules of Civil Procedure.

In support of this request, the plaintiff relies upon the record in this case and the affidavit submitted herein.

This the 25th day of August 2015.

BY: _____

David Thomas Silvers Sr.

UNITED STATES DISTRICT COURT, WESTERN
DISTRICT OF NORTH CAROLINA STATESVILLE
DIVISION

David Thomas Silvers Sr. [pro se] Plaintiff vs. Iredell County Department of Social Services, D.S.S. Dir. Donald Wall, in individual and official capacities; Asst. D.A. Paxton Butler, in individual and official capacities; City of Statesville, N.C. Defendant(s)	CIVIL NO. 5:15CV83-RLV

DEFAULT JUDGMENT

The defendant, Paxton Butler, in individual, and

official capacities for the City of Statesville, N.C., having

failed to plead or otherwise defend in this action, and

default having heretofore been entered; upon

application of plaintiff and upon affidavit that the City of

Statesville, N.C. is indebted to plaintiff in the principal

sum of $13,520,000 plus interest thereon; that

defendant Paxton Butler, in individual, and official

capacities for the City of Statesville, N.C. had been

defaulted for failure to appear pursuant to Rule 55(a) of

the Federal Rules of Civil Procedure; and that the claim

is for a sum certain or for a sum which can by

computation be made certain.

It is hereby ORDERED, ADJUDGED, and

DECREED that plaintiff, David Thomas Silvers Sr.,

recover of the City of Statesville, N.C. the sum of

$13,520,000, plus interest according to law from the

date of this judgment until the entire amount is paid.

This judgment is entered by the Clerk at the

request of the plaintiff and upon affidavit that said

amount is due, in accordance with Rule 55 (b) (1) of the

Federal Rules of Civil Procedure.

BY: _____
Clerk of Court

[1]David Thomas Silvers Sr.

██████████████████

█████████████████

Richard Voorhees, U.S. District Court Judge
U.S. District Court, W.D. NC. Statesville Division
200 W. Broad St., Rm. 303
Statesville, NC. 28677

RE: Status inquiry on 5:15-cv-00083-RLV-DCK

Dear Richard Voorhees,   December 28th 2015

On or about the middle of December 2015, after

calling and inquiring on the status of the

aforementioned case, the Deputy Clerk advised that I

write the Judge or Clerk to inquire upon the status.

After filing a motion for default judgment on August

27th 2015, I called a Deputy Clerk in good faith on

September 3rd 2015 in the attempt to discover timeline

expectations on the proposed order. The Clerk stated

the Judge has to rule upon Motion for Default Judgment

---

[1] DOC 17

before the Clerk can proceed with 55 (b) (1), and it usually takes a couple weeks before a Motion for Default Judgment is ruled upon.

On September 11th 2015, after two weeks from the August 27th 2015 ruling, I sent the enclosed letter certified mail to the current Director of Social Services Yvette Smith because I was concerned the City of Statesville was harassing me and that the District Court might be considering notification. The following should alleviate those concerns:

1.   In Brandon v. Holt, 469 U.S. 464, 471 (1985), the Court stated there is no arguable basis for claiming that the record would support an award of damages against a substituted party, and since the current Director of Social Services, Yvette Smith, was not involved during the time of the substantial damages in the Complaint, then to alleviate similar concerns of Brandon v. Holt, the prior Director, Donald Wall, whom had supervisory

liability during the time of substantial damages was named on the Complaint followed by an arguable basis for claiming the record would support an award of damages.

2.   The first motion filed by James R. Morgan, Jr. of Womble, Carlyle, Sandridge & Rice noted the connection between the Director of Social Services and the City of Statesville, and that was followed by further representation of Meagan L. Kiser of Cranfill, Sumner and Hartzog.

3.   The information in the enclosed letter to Director Yvette Smith demonstrates that Social Services and therefore the City of Statesville was aware of the Complaint after the filing on June 30th 2015 and before the Entry of Default was filed on August 24th 2015.

The other possible question I thought that the Court might be considering is the additional request for punitive damages, and those damage considerations are supported by the following: In City of Newport v.

Fact Concerts, 453 U.S. 247 (1981), the Supreme

Court stated that "punitive damages might be awarded

in appropriate circumstances in order to punish

violations of constitutional rights, Carey v. Piphus, 435

U. S. 247 (1978)". In Carey v. Piphus, 435 U.S. 247,

266 (1978) the Supreme Court stated "it remains true to

the principle that substantial damages should be

awarded only to compensate actual injury or, in the

case of exemplary or punitive damages, to deter or

punish malicious deprivations of rights", and in

Footnote [11] "This is not to say that exemplary or

punitive damages might not be awarded in a proper

case under § 1983 with the specific purpose of

deterring or punishing violations of constitutional rights.

See, e.g., Silver v. Cormier, 529 F.2d 161, 163-164

(CA10 1976);", and in Footnote [22], In Basista v. Weir,

340 F.2d 74 (CA3 1965); Sexton v. Gibbs, 327 F.Supp.

134 (ND Tex.1970), aff'd, 446 F.2d 904 (CA5 1971),

cert. denied, 404 U.S. 1062 (1972); and Rhoads v.

Horvat, 270 F.Supp. 307 (Colo.1967), cited in Hostrop,

supra, at 579, the courts indicated that damages may

be awarded for humiliation and distress caused by

unlawful arrests, searches, and seizures. In Basista v.

Weir, the court held that nominal damages could be

awarded for an illegal arrest even if compensatory

damages were waived, and that such nominal damages

would, in an appropriate case, support an award of

punitive damages. 340 F.2d at 87-88.". In Silver v.

Cormier, 529 F. 2d 161 (1976), the 10th Circuit Court of

Appeals stated "such conduct by a public official

manifests a reckless indifference to the property rights

of others, ill will, a desire to injure or malice. Punitive

damages are recoverable in a section 1983 action

provided such aggravating circumstances are found.

Spence v. Staras, 7 Cir., 507 F.2d 554, 558; Morales v.

Haines, 7 Cir., 486 F.2d 880, 882; Smith v. Lossee, 10

Cir., 485 F.2d 334, 345, cert. denied, 417 U.S. 908, 94

S.Ct. 2604, 41 L.Ed.2d 212; McDaniel v. Carroll, 6 Cir.,

457 F.2d 968, 969, cert. denied, 409 U.S. 1106, 93

S.Ct. 897, 34 L.Ed.2d 687. Recovery of punitive

damages has been held to be permitted in actions

under section 1983 even in the absence of actual loss.

Spence v. Staras, 7 Cir., 507 F.2d 554, 558; Fisher v.

Volz, 164*164 3 Cir., 496 F.2d 333, 346-47; Stolberg v.

Members of Board of Trustees, 2 Cir., 474 F.2d 485,

489; Basista v. Weir, 3 Cir., 340 F.2d 74, 88."

One of the most substantial claims and

continuing concern is the ongoing delays in seeking

justice in this case. The deprivation of rights, injustices,

and excessive delays have caused substantial

damages and impeded improvement of myself, and my

family.

The reason I chose the State of Virginia as a place to relocate is because I was concerned that the U.S. District Court was in the same City I am suing, and that there might be more delays and a possibility of having to write a "Writ of Memorandus" to the Federal Fourth Circuit Court in Richmond, VA to compel action in the U.S. District Court. After researching a "Writ of Memorandus", I discovered the Federal Circuit Courts recommend communicating concerns with the District Court before filing a "Writ of Memorandus". In good faith and with due diligence, I strongly believe that I have alleviated concerns in the District and Circuit Court, and respectfully request an expeditious ruling in this case.

Sincerely,

David Thomas Silvers Sr.

[1]David Thomas Silvers Sr.

██████████████████

David Keesler, U.S. District Court Magistrate
U.S. District Court, W.D. NC. Statesville Division
200 W. Broad St., Rm. 303
Statesville, NC. 28677

RE: Seeking Magistrate support on 5:15-cv-00083-

RLV-DCK

January 4th 2016

Dear David Keesler,

The purpose of this letter is to seek additional

support on aforementioned case and for the December

28th 2015 letter to U.S. District Court Judge Richard

Voorhees.

If the Iredell County Department of Social

Services under supervisory liability of Donald Wall, and

---

[1] DOC. 18

the Assistant District Attorney Paxton Butler, did not interfere, excessively entangle, and coerce with a threat of charges that deliberately obstructed the custody hearing stated in Amended Complaint, it is highly likely that an impartial and reasonable justice would have ruled in the favor of this father from the following facts:

A. The following are this father's influence:

1. Youngest Son: 'A/B' student with perfect attendance and a father and son award in cub scouts while harmless to others.

2. Junior: 'A/B' student with perfect attendance and an extracurricular award while harmless to others.

3. Daughter: after a year in her father's custody, her father made up for her prior flunking in her mother's custody by getting her back into the grade of her peers, and then she earned nine consecutive quarters of straight 'A's with perfect

attendance and earning multiple awards while caring, loving, and helping her father advance his sons while harmless to others.

B. The following are their mother's influence:

1. Youngest: nightmares from unsupervised movies, skipping class and flunking.

2. Junior: skipping class and flunking while receiving complaints from the community watch group while mother told others that junior, whom was an A/B student, had a learning disability and then had junior ungratefully harm by slandering his father on the Court record through a social worker on the stand.

3. Daughter: stealing at school, skipping class and flunking, breach of promise, stripping her down in public as an ungrateful and treacherous prostitute for pimping by mob-rule while ungratefully slandering and harming her father.

The issue with the mother is she wanted the children to relive her childhood when dysfunctional and unstable childhoods with deficiencies in sympathy, empathy, affection, and remorse from a defective conscience can cause psychopathic behavior. The mother had a dysfunctional and unstable childhood whereas she was deficient in how she processed emotions while lacking empathy for the feelings of others, such as not only feelings expressed in poetic writings and drawings, the antisocial behavior of not calling their father nor request any of the children call their father while being hostile to the well-being of others and making the children dysfunctional, unstable, and mentally ill until they ungratefully harmed their father with slander, of which can cause unpredictable consequences and therefore the mother disregarded the safety of others.

The conscience of my children was degenerated by others with a breach of promise and selfish slander while thus far there has been no remorse, and I am concerned that there has not been enough improvement of their psychopathic mentality.

During their father's custody, their father secured their safety with respect for others while there was sympathy, empathy, and affection while solidifying their conscience with obligations and responsibilities, and then my children ascended to their father's standards whereas they were a success in the home, school, and community.

The summation is unconstitutional invasions of privacy, crowding and ganging for ostracizing, potsherd gambling, and salacious profiteering using the fickleness of political vacillations that waste time when advocating ungrateful, treacherous, and irresponsible coercing and brainwashing into a breach of promise

that caused oppression and libelous slander followed
by prosecutorial misconduct with extraneous
interference and deliberate obstruction of justice before
custody hearing where libelous slander was stated on
the public Court record, then a father with a non-
threatening U.S. Constitutional First Amendment
protest followed by depriving rights with excessive
entanglement and unconstitutional charges, then years
of depriving due process, then another protest, then
another unconstitutional charge, then years of depriving
due process, then another protest, then years of
wrongful incarceration while forcing harmful drugs and
depriving due process. The foregoing has caused
substantial burdens and substantial damages when this
father and all of his children were merited prior to the
unconstitutional invasions of privacy by the perverted
degenerates of mob-rule that deprive rights and pander
to lurid curiosity while playing dramatic confidence

games using spurious imposters and goons of State that recklessly disregarded gratefulness, virginity, merit, ethics, and justice; then a redress of grievances, a default, and now more delays in Federal Court. The issue is the opposition has nothing significantly beneficial to substantially stand on while the U.S. Supreme Court has ruled more than once that neutrality was, and is, the State's only course in order to secure unalienable rights such as privacy that prevents totalitarian terrorism from tyranny of the majority.

Sincerely,

_____

David Thomas Silvers Sr.

[1]David Thomas Silvers Sr.

███████████

Frank G. Johns, Clerk of Court
U.S. District Court, W.D. NC. Statesville Division
200 W. Broad St. Rm. 303
Statesville, NC 28677

RE: Default on 5:15-cv-00083-RLV-DCK

Dear Frank G. Johns,   January 27th, 2016

The purpose of this letter is to request due diligence on Federal rules of civil procedure and express the unpredictable consequences of disregarding rules of civil procedure. For example, there was another hearing that the Iredell County Department of Social Services under supervisory liability of Donald Wall attempted to extraneously interfere with, and that was the first hearing in the District Court of Dundalk, Maryland.

---

[1] DOC. 19

A couple weeks prior to the aforementioned hearing, and while my children were visiting in Maryland, and while no one in my family was pursuing criminal charges, the Iredell County Department of Social Services contacted the District Attorney's office as stated in the "Reply Brief Supporting Opposition to Defendant Wall's Motion to Dismiss" to extraneously interfere, excessively entangle, and deliberately obstruct justice before the Maryland hearing, similar to what the Iredell County Department of Social Services did prior to a later hearing stated in the Amended Complaint. Moments prior to the hearing in Dundalk Maryland, I amicably approached my sons and their amicable response demonstrated that they wanted to return in their father's custody. I then had my lawyer argue for their safe return and the judge ruled in my favor. I then walked out of the Courtroom and into the hall of justice to get my sons and their mother's boyfriend recklessly disregarded justice and rules of

civil procedure, then kidnapped my sons by grabbing

them and running out of the Courthouse - exemplifying

how mob-rule is a rough sea for the ship of State to ride

- I then followed him outside and he aggressively

interpolated them into his vehicle and aggressively

moved in the direction of their father. At that moment

my lawyer got between myself and the mother's

boyfriend, and then we went back into the Courtroom

and the judge sent the matter to the higher Baltimore

County Circuit Court to be heard at a later date. When I

went home my first thought from my indignation was

getting a gun and executing the mother's boyfriend for

his lack of respect and injustice when prior I had never

thought about killing anyone in my life.

The mother and her boyfriend distracted others

into pandering my daughter that they harmed and found

many intruders with perverted curiosities or salacious

interests to deprive rights and pander to lurid curiosity, when a year prior the mother's boyfriend had attempted to turn my sons against their father since he only sired girls without siring sons, and then wanted my sons and sought out illegitimate interests to invalidate trade.

The reason I stayed the execution is because I had good faith that a competent justice system would resolve this matter expeditiously, however, I discovered that salacious profiteers have influenced modern politicians into disregarding privacy while arguing against the free exercise of religion in U.S. Constitutional First and Fourteenth Amendments, and gun rights in the Second Amendment that can restrain and refrain trespassers, whom can also be public officials from the State when there is no respect for separation of powers resulting in a modern State becoming the tyranny that deprives rights and forces their way into another's house using illegitimate arguments, illegal searches, illegal seizures, and illegal arrests while wasting the time and merit of others.

After discovering the inadequacies of extraneous modern politics that advocate a deprivation of rights with excessive delays in serving justice, then if I knew then that a decade later I would be enslaved into serving modern ignorance after I was already favored in the highest Courts in a State with custody and a promise, and amicably mitigated with favor moments before the kidnapping, then I would have immediately executed their mother's boyfriend. It is highly likely another potent, experienced, skillful, and reasonable father that is prudently presiding over his tactfully stable, experienced, and merited family before invasions of privacy would agree; therefore there is adequate support, especially after incompetent intruders coercively turn stable, healthy, happy, successful, and harmless into the antonyms: unstable, unhealthy, hatred, flunking, and harming when relying on mob-rule and jeopardy by coercing in a State of ignorance with laws of irony when advocating a flunking and unmarried 13 year old to lose her virginity to a non-committal 13-15 year old rather than respecting a 15 year old straight 'A' virgin; therefore the straight 'A' virgin is better off with discipline and support of a religious convent while respectfully and confidently learning the stability and integrity of morals, values, and promises rather than ungratefully, ignorantly, coercively, treacherously, and irresponsibly stripped down in public as a slanderous prostitute for pimping by mob-rule while degenerating others in the potently stable, healthy, happy, successful, and harmless family; therefore his sons should have been returned in their father's custody before being kidnapped and brainwashed into slandering their father, and when there is now more than a five million women surplus, their father could care for his daughter and his daughter could care for her father until death do they part without harming others.

The impotent, unskillful, inexperienced, insensible, insensitive, tactless, intrusive, malicious, aggressive, and extrajudicial commentators and shrinks that invade privacy and aggravate with discrimination from a lack of respect for cultural diversity and the dignity of the citizenry - especially when the merited results were better prior to visiting another State - think the justice system is a game when a game cannot be played without rules of civil procedure. It is also important to realize that many men do not want to play games of conjecture, inaction, and injustice with trespassers that ambiguously argue in his house, refuse to agree to disagree then refuse to leave the premises; followed by enslaved into paying taxes to an interfering, entangling, slandering, and corrupt City. The public officials named on the Complaint for the City of Statesville, N.C. were prejudiced, discriminatory, lacked tactful communication skills, and deprived rights.

When there are no respected rules of civil procedure there is only vigilantism leaving only hope that the self-doer of justice is competent enough to adequately serve justice. In this situation, I have had clemency and mercy on others multiple times and now request additional support from a U.S. District Court Judge, Magistrate, and Clerk.

Sincerely,

_____

David Thomas Silvers Sr.

[1]David Thomas Silvers Sr.

███████████████

███████████████

Richard Voorhees, U.S. District Court Judge
U.S. District Court, W.D. NC. Statesville Division
200 W. Broad St., Rm. 303
Statesville, NC. 28677

RE: Order of February 3rd 2016 on 5:15-cv-00083-RLV-DCK

Dear Richard Voorhees,   February 10th 2016

The purpose of this letter is to first, as a pro se

plaintiff, thank you for the latitude; second, inform that I

respectfully decline to file a suggested second

Amendment that would effectively restart the lawsuit

and permit the defaulted defendant more than six

months to respond to what should have been

responded to in 21 days; third, without a second

Amendment, then that might not give me an opportunity

---

[1] DOC. 21

to correct and set the record straight after you misinterpreted the first Amended Complaint referenced in your last Order dated February 3rd 2016; fourth, communicate my willingness to proceed with a request for summary judgement, or continue against the other defendant and entities since it appears you have served other officials to ensure without doubt that Iredell County and the City of Statesville is aware and have been notified of the lawsuit.

Prior to responding with specificity to your last Order, I was, and still am, hoping that the last three letters I sent this U.S. District Court was adequate enough to answer most of the cites for punitive damages that I cited in my last letter to you. I am now uncertain if your suggestion for another Amendment was intended for facilitating the incorporating of some information from the aforementioned letters, however, if it was not several months after default I might consider arguments from the defaulted defendant. After considering the information in the letter sent to the Clerk, the only undisclosed information that is useful is what happened in the Baltimore County Circuit Court on August 12th 2004 where Social Services in Maryland attempted to make an argument, however, to counter belatedly unrefined discrimination "under color of state law" from sleazy gossiping trash of Social Services that were trying to interfere and entangle, the Circuit Court Judge asked only one question, and that question was "how are the children doing in school", and after my lawyer responded "good", the Judge wanted to ensure they were doing good and sent the matter to the Courts in Statesville, North Carolina, however, Iredell County D.S.S. continued interfering and entangling while participating in the underachieving and belatedly unrefined discriminating with sleazy slanderous trash. You might have referred to "sleazy trash" in the

Amended Complaint, and some words sent to the Magistrate as 'inartful', however, when no other words accurately describe the aftermath then the foregoing words should be acknowledged.

1. Order page 2: Regarding my children, "Plaintiff does not allege who was coerced, how such person(s) were coerced, or for what purpose such person(s) were "coerced".

Response: Intended for inference of my three youngest children that visited their mother while "how" and for "what" is conjecture since I was not present during her unsupervised visitations, although, coercion is a reasonable conclusion since my sons wanted to return in their father's custody after first visitation with father, and until unsupervised visitations with their mother that was followed by slander in the civil custody hearing.

2. Order page 3: "Defendant Butler threatened Plaintiff's counsel"

Response: Defendant Butler threatened Plaintiff through counsel.

3. Order page 4: "The First Amended Complaint does not allege whether Plaintiff was ever tried or convicted of these charges"

Response: A reasonable inference from a deprivation of due process claim with factually stated protests in the Amended Complaint is that there was no trial nor conviction nor substantive due process, only dismissal.

4. Order page 4: regarding "fraudulently burning dwelling" ..."Plaintiff does not allege whether he was convicted of this charge, or whether this charge was dropped".

Response: The inference from the above response to item 3 also applies to item 4.

5. Order page 4: "the First Amended Complaint does not allege whether the detention resulted from any of the above mentioned charges, whether it occurred as the result of a trial or plea, or whether it resulted from some sort of civil detention or guardianship"

Response: The inference from above is not as transparent, however, due to the prior protests stated in Amended Complaint, a reasonable inference is that all subsequent actions by plaintiff were a pattern of protests. After several years of attending roll call without substantive due process for any of the charges, the record in the Superior Court of Iredell County should show that incarceration was for a no show for roll call from my belief that incarceration would expedite substantive due process since there are more laws and rulings regarding excessive amount of incarcerated time without due process.

6. Order page 4: "Plaintiff does not allege who improperly sent him back 'back and forth' to this 'mental institution' and who forced him to take harmful drugs".

Response: The issue with U.S. Supreme Court rulings regarding civil lawsuits against Government entities is that the lawsuit can only be brought against a County or City while excluding State, and since the mental institution is run by the State, employees for the State seem to have immunity to conjecture and force harmful drugs in citizens, similar to genocidal practices of WWII Germany; therefore 'who' is most likely granted immunity while it is my hope that in regards to State mental Institutions that future laws, and rulings from the U.S. Supreme Court, declare a State can be held liable, and that harmless citizens are safe in the future from the coercive acts of totalitarian terrorism.

7. Order page 24: In addition to the response from above item 2, and on page 24: "Plaintiff was still free to participate in the proceedings sans counsel".

Response: When on the day and in the moments prior to a civil custody hearing, and when at that time a father has minimal legal expertise, finds that he is against a State prosecutor outside the hearing threatening charges through counsel, and then with no time to review the Statute(s), or opportunity for continuance, and when in the hearing is a D.S.S. attorney, Ad Litem attorney, and mother's attorney, then a reasonable person can conclude that without religion, the odds are stacked against a father, and that there was a coercive denial of adequate, effective, and meaningful access to the civil hearing.

8. Order page 24: "Plaintiff did participate in the hearing".

Response: seated behind the rail and in the audience as a spectator in a Courtroom does not validate participation in the hearing. It means remain silent or go to jail.

9. Order page 25: "the First Amended Complaint also does not allege that Defendant Butler's actions deprived Plaintiff of any available state law remedies, such as an appeal or his right to seek a modification of custodial rights."

Response: After a State of subjugations, many modern fathers would walk away from ungrateful, treacherous, slanderous, and unmerited children while my response was to merely express freedom of speech in writing a few months later that was followed by an illegal arrest from unconstitutional invasions of privacy and unconstitutional charges.

10. Order page 27: "writings were presented to the grand jury"

Response: I never stated I knew what was presented to the grand jury, I only stated the defendant Butler did not provide any exculpatory information from my religious writing.

11. Order page 30: regarding "fraudulently burning a dwelling charge": "the first Amended Complaint fails to cite any authority for these legal assertions".

Response: I cited multiple U.S. Constitutional Amendments that counter the above charge, and like the North Carolina Supreme Court, I am sure that U.S. Constitutional Amendments and U.S. Supreme Court rulings thereof were used as their authority.

12. Order page 30: regarding International Human Rights: "Plaintiff's First Amended Complaint fails to cite

this Court to any treaty or executive agreement of the
United States that affords Plaintiff rights."

Response: Since 1945, all of the International Human
Rights treaties have been accepted and sanctioned by
the United States, and without respecting the quote in
the Amended Complaint from the foregoing precepts,
then it is unlikely there will be an executive agreement
from a modern Democracy of fascism. In the modern
era, and before Barack Obama was elected President,
Barack Obama advocated "strip mining" in his
published book when strip mining is what coalesces
into a wearisome exposition that can degenerate others
when relying on the underachieving and unrefined
many.

CONCLUSION

It appears from your ruling that multiple U.S. Constitution Amendments should be shredded in favor of modern day mob-rule while bringing America back to the Civil War era or turning Americans into the Germans of WWII. In this situation, the public officials named on the Complaint for the State of North Carolina, County of Iredell, and/or City of Statesville of where I resided and therefore primarily liable, are no better than the illegitimacy of the mother's boyfriend - mentioned in my letter to the Clerk on 1/27/2016 - that disregarded justice in the District Court of Dundalk, Maryland, then coercively kidnapped and brainwashed my children into an ungrateful, unmerited, dysfunctional, treacherous, and slanderous oppression. A father's sired children are not the property of the State for subjugation in the home and in the workplace, and a man's identity and character is not built upon the capricious vicissitudes and fickleness of popular public belated opinion. When there are different circumstances and no respect for different material traits, different races, different religions, and different social groups without invidious discrimination, and the cultural diversity with distinct forms that secure thereof with dignity for the citizenry, then without private property and right of privacy there is only coercing in a unilateral culture and unilateral form of tyranny that has, can, and will result in genocidal tendencies and oppression in another group. The way to ensure domestic tranquility without subjugation is not strip mining, it is by respecting cultural diversity with distinct forms that are secured by private property and privacy rights.

Sincerely,

_____

David Thomas Silvers Sr.

[1]David Thomas Silvers Sr.

███████████████████

Frank G. Johns, Clerk of Court
U.S. District Court, W.D. NC. Statesville Division
200 W. Broad St. Rm. 303
Statesville, NC 28677

RE: 5:15-cv-00083-RLV-DCK – for the Court record.

Dear Frank G. Johns,   April 6th 2016

INJUSTICES

1. Mother is anti-social and fails to call father.

2. Mother harms daughter using barbarism.

3. Mother's boyfriend disregards judge's order and rules of civil procedure then coercively kidnaps father's sons.

4. Director of Social Services is not politically correct, neglects a Circuit Court Order and then barbarically strip mines.

---

[1] DOC. 35

5. Statesville NC justice system is not politically correct and orders unfair visitations.

6. Assistant District Attorney is not politically correct and coerces a threat of charges if participating in custody hearing.

7. Testimony by social worker under oath with slander from third party hearsay is admitted into record.

8. Assistant District Attorney neglects the free exercise of religion and freedom of speech in a protest writing claiming slander, and a police investigator that believes there is slanderous statements by the alleged victim, then charges.

9. Assistant District Attorney neglects NC Supreme Court and NC Circuit Court rulings and then presses another charge without substantial harm to another's property nor a claim to fraudulently collect insurance.

10. Nearly 4 years of incarceration and more than 7 years without due process.

11. Forcing harmful drugs by a State mental institution.

12. Assistant District Attorney fails to respond to complaint.

13. Federal Judge denies default judgment.

14. Federal Judge is negligent with reckless indifference to the foregoing injustices and describes the Amended Complaint using a linguistic barbarism that implies he advocates strip mining and inner-city strip clubs whereas a reasonable person of a relatively high level of cultural development can conclude the justice system in Statesville NC is unjust, inferior, degenerate, disgraceful, and uncivilized.

Sincerely,

_____

David Thomas Silvers Sr.

No. 16-1549

UNITED STATES COURT OF APPEALS FOR THE FOURTH CIRCUIT

DAVID THOMAS SILVERS SR.

Plaintiff-Appellant

vs.

IREDELL COUNTY DEPARTMENT OF SOCIAL

SERVICES, D.S.S. DIR. DONALD WALL, IN

INDIVIDUAL AND OFFICIAL CAPACITIES, ASST. D.A.

PAXTON BUTLER, IN INDIVIDUAL AND OFFICIAL

CAPACITIES, AND THE CITY OF STATESVILLE,

NORTH CAROLINA

Defendants-Appellees

On Appeal from the United States District Court for the

Western District of North Carolina, Statesville Division

Case No. 5:15-cv-00083-RLV-DCK

APPELLANT'S INFORMAL BRIEF

TABLE OF CONTENTS

STATEMENT OF JURISDICTION

The plaintiff filed a Complaint in the United States District Court for the Western District of North Carolina, Statesville Division on June 30th 2015, followed by filing an Amended Complaint on July 21st 2015 as a civil action under 42 U.S.C §1983 and §1985 for acts committed by defendants under color of state law which deprived plaintiff of security, privacy, liberty, and property without due process of law and in violation of the First, Fourth, Fifth, and Fourteenth Amendments of the United States Constitution, and International Human Rights. Review is sought of an Order that is against the plaintiff-appellant signed by United States District judge Richard Voorhees on April 15th 2016, and since the foregoing Order referenced his prior Order dated on February 3rd 2016, a review is sought for both of the foregoing Orders.

STATEMENT OF THE ISSUES

1. Whether plaintiff-appellant has the rights declared in the Amended Complaint, and whether any of the plaintiff's rights were violated by any of the defendants on the Amended Complaint then neglected and erred by the Federal District judge.

2. Whether the Federal District judge erred in not granting the motion for default judgement.

3. Whether the statute of limitation argument is valid under Silvers v. Iredell County Department of Social Services et al., 5:15-CV-00083 after the defendants conspired with one another and the injury continued.

ARGUMENT

The plaintiff-appellant believes he has the rights declared in the Amended Complaint and is entitled to the relief sought in the Amended Complaint while the plaintiff does not believe the statute of limitation argument is valid under Silvers v. Iredell County Department of Social Services et al., 5:15-cv-00083, especially after the spurious and unconstitutional charges that relied on invasions of privacy and linguistic barbarism that was conspired between both defendants on the Amended Complaint, see also: Silvers v. Iredell County Department of Social Services et al., 5:15-cv-00083, Reply Brief Supporting Opposition to Defendant Wall's Motion to Dismiss, whereas since the Iredell County N.C. Department of Social Services, hereafter I.C.N.C.D.S.S., has attempted to undermine religion and the stability of families, then if I.C.N.C.D.S.S. of the County or City does not maintain the same privacy separation of Church and State, then their collusion

with the State can be considered as a conspiracy to

deprive the right of privacy from the separation of

Church and State, and when a Church is in question,

and then after debate from James Madison with his

fellow men of which Church, and when not all of his

fellow men agreed on only one Church, then James

Madison expressed the free exercise of religion "as he

believes to be acceptable to him", Amended Complaint

pg. 3, of which after a psychoanalysis of extraneous

and modern social stigmas from invidious discrimination

among other groups, James Madison can be

paraphrased with what a father believes in real time is

an acceptable pattern for his sons, of which in plaintiff's

family was with a regular religious order by the plaintiff

as father whereas father and daughter were the

Church, and father and sons were the State while their

father reserved a right of privacy in both groups with a

result of healthy tranquility and merited achievements

with refinement and signatures from plaintiff's sons.

When the foregoing privacy separation worked on

private property, then that privacy separation can work

in a Country. After evaluating others conjecture on what

could have happened regarding the father and daughter

relationship without invasions of privacy, the plaintiff

honestly did not know what could have happened since

that decision involved two sincerely caring for one

another and empathizing with one another to make a

final decision, and when that decision was already

made with a statement by plaintiff's daughter of "we feel

the same way" and a promise followed by signatures

from plaintiff's sons, then that decision is an absolute

binder reality. After others invaded privacy then they

can be considered as sleazy trash and insincere

thieves, Amended Complaint pg. 7. The issue from the

invasions of privacy is that others continued asking

plaintiff's daughter "what did he say" or "what did he do", when what the plaintiff said and what the plaintiff did was mostly in response to what the plaintiff's daughter said or did in order to maintain domestic tranquility and her scholastic achievements. It was one of the better relationships the plaintiff experienced, although, since at that time the plaintiff's daughter did not experience many relationships in her life, and then after she went through a harsh inquisition from others, she gossiped while mixing in lies from what others wanted to hear when the plaintiff knew that eventually, after plaintiff's daughter experienced other relationships later in life, she would realize the value of her father and daughter relationship while the defendants conspired with one another and gambled on the opposite while the public officials and authorities for the City of Statesville left the plaintiff incarcerated thinking the plaintiff's daughter would realize the value of another relationship then ungratefully testify against her father when regardless of which relationship is better, turning family members against one another is not generally accepted, and since I.C.N.C.D.S.S. and the City of Statesville guessed wrong with their conjecture, they should compensate the plaintiff as stated in the Amended Complaint for the injury of which also prevents others from being charged and incarcerated from victimless conjecture and without substantive due process, regardless if the interfering and antagonism was started by their mother whom was psychopathically hostile to the well-being and used oppression on daughter. The County, City, and State interfered, antagonized, and caused oppression on their father by belatedly, negligently, extraneously, and excessively entangling the free exercise of religion with barbarously profane invasions of privacy, Amended Complaint pg. 2, 3, and 7. Moreover, before the expiration of the N.C.

three year statute of limitation period, the spurious,

genocidal, and totalitarian charges, Amended

Complaint pg. 4, led to invoking the Fourteenth, First,

and Fifth U.S. Constitutional Amendments for the right

of privacy, especially when there was a sacred promise

before the invasions of privacy while thereof is a

reasonable expectation of privacy, see also: Silvers v.

I.C.N.C.D.S.S. et al., 5:15-cv-00083, Plaintiff's

Opposition to Defendant Wall's Renewed Motion to

Dismiss, and Brief in Support of Plaintiff's Opposition to

Defendant Wall's Renewed Motion to Dismiss. The

Federal District Court judge could have used the statute

of limitation argument in his first Order whereas a

request for another Amendment would not have

changed the dates of incarceration nor the last date

from a continuous injury; therefore, ulterior motive

and/or incompetence of the Federal District Court judge

can be reasonably inferred, especially with his

dismissal of multiple U.S. Constitutional Right claims and an International Human Rights claim in his first Order while that incompetence inference was already decided against the judges of tyranny of the majority during the Nuremberg Germany trials in 1946. Moreover, in his last Order, the judge used the following statement of irony: "The Court granted Plaintiff leave to file a second Amended Complaint in attempt to cure his deficiencies", whereas now there is a need to not only restate the injustice of being impelled to restart the case and give the defaulted defendant more than six months to respond to the Amended Complaint, see: Silvers v. I.C.N.C.D.S.S. et al., 5:15-cv-00083, entry 21 pg. 1, also counter his use of the word deficient by relating the definition of deficient: "Lacking something necessary; not up to normal standard" whereas normal is: "not conforming to a type, standard, or regular pattern". What is necessary is sustenance that was provided by

the plaintiff while the Amended Complaint used a

settled lawsuit of Dail v. City of Goldsboro,

5:2010cv00451 U.S. District Court, E.D. N.C. Western

Division, as a template type with the addition of

including specific U.S. Constitutional Amendments in

each numbered paragraph that conforms to the Federal

Fourth Circuit Court decision in Evans v. Chalmers, 703

F. 3d 636, 2012. On page 1 of the Amended Complaint,

the plaintiff also referred to a type from the Baltimore

County Circuit Court of Maryland and the Supreme

Court of Maryland in favor of the plaintiff that proceeded

with a regular religious order that was respectfully

arranged with a care first mentality of "sincere

providence", Amended Complaint pg. 3, and

Declaration of Independence (1776), and an Edwardian

pattern with well-being considerations and no

substantial harm to others, of which is highly likely

respected and accepted among the 50 United States;

therefore, the foregoing can also conform to the 10th Amendment of the U.S. Constitution. On page two of the Amended Complaint there are the following type cite standards regarding privacy: "relating to marriage procreation, contraception, family relationships, and child rearing and education", Paul v. Davis, 424 U.S. 693 (1976), and International Human Rights that prohibits "interfering with his privacy, family, home or correspondence, nor attacks upon his honor and reputation", and Monell v. Department of Soc. Serv. 436 U.S. 658 (1978). In addition, there are the following type cites in Silvers v. I.C.N.C.D.S.S. et al., 5:15-cv-00083, entry 17, pg. 2: In City of Newport v. Fact Concerts, 453 U.S. 247 (1981), the Supreme Court stated that "punitive damages might be awarded in appropriate circumstances in order to punish violations of constitutional rights, Carey v. Piphus, 435 U. S. 247 (1978)". In Carey v. Piphus, 435 U.S. 247, 266 (1978) the Supreme Court stated "it remains true to the

principle that substantial damages should be awarded

only to compensate actual injury or, in the case of

exemplary or punitive damages, to deter or punish

malicious deprivations of rights", and in Footnote [11]

"This is not to say that exemplary or punitive damages

might not be awarded in a proper case under § 1983

with the specific purpose of deterring or punishing

violations of constitutional rights. See, e.g., Silver v.

Cormier, 529 F.2d 161, 163-164 (CA10 1976);", and in

Footnote [22], In Basista v. Weir, 340 F.2d 74 (CA3

1965); Sexton v. Gibbs, 327 F.Supp. 134 (ND

Tex.1970), aff'd, 446 F.2d 904 (CA5 1971), cert.

denied, 404 U.S. 1062 (1972); and Rhoads v. Horvat,

270 F.Supp. 307 (Colo.1967), cited in Hostrop, supra,

at 579, the courts indicated that damages may be

awarded for humiliation and distress caused by

unlawful arrests, searches, and seizures. In Basista v.

Weir, the court held that nominal damages could be awarded for an illegal arrest even if compensatory damages were waived, and that such nominal damages would, in an appropriate case, support an award of punitive damages. 340 F.2d at 87-88.". In Silver v. Cormier, 529 F. 2d 161 (1976), the 10th Circuit Court of Appeals stated "such conduct by a public official manifests a reckless indifference to the property rights of others, ill will, a desire to injure or malice. Punitive damages are recoverable in a section 1983 action provided such aggravating circumstances are found. Spence v. Staras, 7 Cir., 507 F.2d 554, 558; Morales v. Haines, 7 Cir., 486 F.2d 880, 882; Smith v. Lossee, 10 Cir., 485 F.2d 334, 345, cert. denied, 417 U.S. 908, 94 S.Ct. 2604, 41 L.Ed.2d 212; McDaniel v. Carroll, 6 Cir., 457 F.2d 968, 969, cert. denied, 409 U.S. 1106, 93 S.Ct. 897, 34 L.Ed.2d 687. The reason for most of plaintiff's concern in the initial aftermath was the negligence and coercive threat of charges by Paxton

Butler with I.C.N.C.D.S.S that did not want the plaintiff

to discredit the mother in the custody hearing followed

by slander stated under oath of which does not help the

plaintiff's children nor anyone else, and if they thought it

did, there conscience will not help them in the future

while after the custody hearing there were many that

thought the plaintiff should have publically humiliated

his family in Court rather than sincerely grieve while the

Federal District Court judge barbarously and ironically

implied the grievance should be from a violin when the

grieving that others observed in the custody hearing

was for junior whom was misled into slander by his

mother and his grandmother whom as a mother could

not prevent her fatherless teenage son from overdosing

on the inner-city streets. The public Court systems that

make an attempt at honor, are only reactive to the

people whom are injured within their jurisdiction, and

have proven to be less worthy and less honorable than a proactive father with a biological predisposition and daily insight that keeps his family safe and secure and the families around him safe and secure, and when fathers start becoming injured from invasions of privacy, then that will result in more injuries of not only fathers and their families, many others; for example, there are more fatherless people in the City with a result of an excessive murder rate in the City while the salacious interests of densely populated Cities have excessive divorce rates and are more interested in pandering and pimping by mob-rule; therefore, the public Court system needs more advisement from fathers rather than mothers. The plaintiff initially chose freedom of speech in a private religious patristic type writing that reprimanded their mother and corrected the plaintiff's son from slanderous statements that were testified under oath by a social worker from a writing from his grandmother that alleged the plaintiff's son made the slanderous statements, of which was third party slanderous hearsay admitted on the Court record, and then after public distribution of the private religious patristic type writing that was not intended for distribution to the plaintiff's family nor the general public, there was another betrayal with that betrayal from Paxton Butler whom three months earlier stated that if the plaintiff did not participate in the custody hearing there would not be any charges and then charged the plaintiff while vacillating from mother to son and stating to plaintiff's lawyer whom was a crony of Paxton Butler with a conflict of interest thereof, that he was looking out for the son when his representation and the representation of the next lawyer the plaintiff fired were inadequate, just like most of the North Carolina bar association, when again, slander does not help anyone, and for those that thought it did, their conscience will not help them in the future. I discovered that the Statesville, North Carolina justice system was rigged similar to the New Testament from an impotent illusion of coercing people into a delusion of believing that without a father's biological predisposition, daily insight, and merited achievements the degenerative intruders have a higher authority while corrupting the population by advocating adultery and slander from an unskillful socialistic welfare-state of momma's boys that lead to the extremes of salacious profiteering, excessive divorce and murder rates, and communistic economic policies. After being charged and the honor, integrity, merit, and reputation that the plaintiff had built was at risk by degenerative intruders corrupting not only the plaintiff's children, the general population, and then after a decade of continuous injury the real lawsuit began in earnest, and then after Paxton Butler defaulted, the City of Statesville also defaulted since it was the police from the City of Statesville that

proceeded from others bad faith with an unlawful arrest,

and then when the Federal District judge unjustly

removed Paxton Butler from liability consideration there

was no choice except to express all the injustices in all

of the entries in Silvers v. I.C.N.C.D.S.S. et al. 5:2015-

cv-00083, and herein, especially since "We the People",

U.S. Constitution (1787), as groups of families and

individual citizens cannot "insure domestic tranquility",

supra, and Silvers v. I.C.N.C.D.S.S. et al., 5:15-cv-

00083 entry 21 pg. 4, while civilized without respecting

religion from the Bible that we put our hands on and

sworn to tell the truth in order to secure our safe

freedom from fear and danger. In addition, religion and

State supports a father and sons with skillful trade and

perhaps multiple wives in conjunction with census

gender arithmetic, Amended Complaint, pg. 6, rather

than the fickle, capricious, unskillful, uncivilized, and

vacillating voters of mob-rule with I.C.N.C.D.S.S. The opposite of morality and merit with religion and State is I.C.N.C.D.S.S. preferring a betrayal from an adulteress running off with another man while I.C.N.C.D.S.S. subjugates the biological father, and if the biological father earns a substantial amount, then in addition to paying a share of taxes for use of public property, the State's excessive child support guidelines compel payment for not only his ungrateful children, the excessive amount pays the treacherous adulteress and her impotent boyfriend. Inevitably fathers will express the deprivation of rights and "secure our rights", Declaration of Independence (1776), before his sons sire as fathers and are compelled by a socialistic welfare-state into becoming slaves, and if their rights are not secured then they will rebel with a revolution, and like the American Revolution, referred to as from the founding fathers, there will be no voting from women with I.C.N.C.D.S.S that can stop the revolution of guns from fathers to their sons; therefore, and as stated in writings to the Federal District Court, Silvers v. I.C.N.C.D.S.S. et al. 5:2015-cv-00083 entry 19, 33, and 35, the plaintiff also supports the right to bear arms in the Second Amendment of the U.S. Constitution, since while there is some respect for the New Testament when respecting a virgin, opposing a betrayal and gambling in the synagogues, there is more respect for the Old Testament that supports the biological father with a promise rather than a spurious imposter as a belated step-father. The issue with the New Testament is that it starts with an unscientific and impotent misconception from an illusion that can be considered as a delusion from a minority of the population for when there is no biological father in the house while the New Testament and the free exercise of religion in the First Amendment of the U.S. Constitution grants a man to become a step-father after marrying the mother. The irony is their mother's boyfriend needed the free exercise of religion more than the biological father, since the biological father should always be the majority of the population with more substantial significance in the Country and State rather than a spurious imposter. When the New Testament becomes preferred over the Old Testament then there is only a fatherless momma's boy of Jesus advocating a communistic economic policy whereas Jesus stated that if person 'A' works 8 hours, and person 'B' works 4 hours, and person 'C' works 2 hours, Jesus states that everyone gets paid the same followed by cleansing the feet of a prostitute, and then Jesus was later executed by the virtue of his fellow countrymen whom did not like his communistic economic policy nor a prostitute, and then after there was continued contention from others teaching only the New Testament, there was separation of orthodox

Churches and unorthodox Churches in the Byzantine

Empire. There was also separation of the Church of

England and Lutheran Church, then more Churches

later separated with their interpretations of both the Old

and the New Testaments, of which is similar to

separations of a separate station in the Declaration of

Independence and separation of powers in the U.S.

Constitution, and separation of religion and State in the

First Amendment of the U.S. Constitution while

interpreting from either the Old Testament or New

Testament, or refinement of both Testaments, and then

after some States abused their authority and refused to

abolish slavery, there was a need to separate people in

the State by securing separate property in the

Fourteenth Amendment. Those that are uneducated in

separation are doomed to repeat history while the hope

is that we do not return to an unseparated and

socialistic State of slavery, or socialistic nationalists of

genocide such as the WWII Germans driven by
extraneous rhetoric when "mob-rule is a rough sea
for the ship of state to ride, every wind of oratory stirs
up the waters and deflects the course" - Plato. The
plaintiff found that the founding fathers of America, and
Abraham Lincoln with the Republican Party wisely built
in separation like the plaintiff prudently built separation
in his family with successful results until sleazy trash
and barbarously profane plunderers belatedly invaded
privacy while upholding only the New Testament and in
denial of their degenerative perversions; therefore,
when the New Testament becomes the majority, then
that majority will become the minority after biological
fathers work together from their real majority and
secure our rights.

CONCLUSION

For the foregoing reasons, the plaintiff respectfully requests this Court reverse the Federal District Court's April 15th 2016 Order granting Defendant Wall's Motion to Dismiss and dismissing with prejudice the plaintiff's First Amended Complaint, reinstate the First Amended Complaint, and the default judgment or return case with corrections to the Federal District Court with a request for another Federal District Court judge.

This the 1st day of June 2016

BY: _____

David Thomas Silvers Sr.

David Thomas Silvers Sr.

██████████████

Clerk of Court
United States Supreme Court
1 First Street, North East
Washington, DC 20543.

Dear Clerk of Court,   November 8th, 2016

Enclosed is a "Petition for Writ of Certiorari" after a judgment on October 17th, 2016 from the United States Court of Appeals for the Fourth Circuit, No. 16-1549, against petitioner that now requests review of the lower courts contravention of the United States Constitution and Amendments, and Rules 10(a)(c) of the Supreme Court of the United States. The "Certificate of Compliance", "Certificate of Service", and a personal check of $300.00 for the docket fee are also enclosed.

Sincerely,

_____

David Thomas Silvers Sr.

No. _____

===

In The

Supreme Court of the United States

DAVID THOMAS SILVERS SR. pro se

Petitioner,

v.

IREDELL COUNTY DEPARTMENT OF SOCIAL

SERVICES, D.S.S. DIR. DONALD WALL, in individual

and official capacities, ASST. D.A. PAXTON BUTLER,

in individual and official capacities, AND

THE CITY OF STATESVILLE, NORTH CAROLINA

Respondents.

On Petition for Writ of Certiorari

To The Federal Fourth Circuit Court

PETITION FOR WRIT OF CERTIORARI

David Thomas Silvers Sr. pro se

QUESTIONS PRESENTED FOR REVIEW

1. Did the Federal District Court err when arguing the case for the defaulted defendant in his Orders while not granting plaintiff relief and judgment against the defaulted defendant then burden the Appeal on the plaintiff rather than on the defaulted Defendant?

2. Did the Federal Fourth Circuit Court err when not considering the merits?

3. Did the Federal Fourth Circuit Court err when not considering important legal principles?

4. Did the Federal Fourth Circuit Court err when not discovering an irreversible error on the record, and in a manner that conflicts with a prior decision of the United States Supreme Court?

5. After considering the following statements and the foregoing points, did the Federal Fourth Circuit Court err when depriving an opportunity for oral arguments?

TABLE OF CONTENTS

TABLE OF AUTHORITIES

CONSTITUTIONAL PROVISIONS, TREATIES,

RULES AND REGULATIONS

42 U.S.C §1983 and §1985

First U.S. Constitutional Amendment

Second U.S. Constitutional Amendment

Fourth U.S. Constitutional Amendment

Fifth U.S. Constitutional Amendment

Fourteenth U.S. Constitutional Amendment

Federal Rules of Civil Procedure 55 (b) (1)

STATEMENT OF JURISDICTION

The Petitioner as Plaintiff filed a Complaint in the United States District Court for the Western District of North Carolina, Statesville Division on June 30, 2015, followed by filing an Amended Complaint on July 21, 2015 as a Civil Action under 42 U.S.C §1983 and §1985 for acts committed by Defendants under color of state law which deprived Petitioner of security, privacy, liberty, and property sans due process of law and in violation of the First, Fourth, Fifth, and Fourteenth Amendments of the United States Constitution, and International Human Rights. Review is sought of an Order that is against the Petitioner signed by United States District judge Richard Voorhees on April 15, 2016, and since the foregoing Order referenced his prior Order dated on February 3, 2016, a review is sought for both of the foregoing Orders and the docket record. On October 17, 2016 a judgment was filed against Petitioner as plaintiff-appellant in the Federal

Fourth Circuit Court before the Circuit Court Judges

Niemeyer, Duncan, and Wynn. The petitioner now files

in opposition a writ of certiorari in the Supreme Court of

the United States.

STATEMENT OF CASE

Other than what has already been stated on the record and corrected herein, most of the oral argument considerations in <u>Appx III</u> were mostly finished and copyrighted on September 25, 2016 then sent for suggestions on October 30, 2016 to the newspaper: Statesville Record and Landmark – through the email address alert@statesville.com – in the City of where I filed a civil action against in Statesville, N.C. The reason that document is included in <u>Appx III</u> is because that document could have been forwarded to the Federal Fourth Circuit Court before the Federal Fourth Circuit Court made an unpublished judgment while at the same time, the following email that accompanied the document might not have been forwarded.

EMAIL: *As a prior resident of the City of Statesville with land and record I believe I should include the freedom of speech with the local press of* the City of Statesville, North Carolina prior to oral arguments against the representatives of the City of Statesville in case 5:15-cv-00083-RLV-DCK in the Federal District Court of Statesville and case 16-1549 in the Federal Fourth Circuit Court of Virginia of where I reside for mitigating and maintaining peaceful relations locally and in the region. Please review the foregoing attached document and let us consider suggestions among one another before locally or nationally publishing our opinions. Note that the Cities should have insurance to cover these lawsuits as to not excessively burden local taxpayers.

Sincerely,

David Thomas Silvers Sr.

The rest of the arguments that were banished are as follows:

In the aftermath after others invaded privacy and then questioned my aspirations, then after privacy considerations, I stated my aspiration would be a position as the Chief Justice of the United States Supreme Court when the foregoing aspiration was thought of more than a decade ago while others only wanted to elect a President when I could be considered as a chief justice after being favored in the Maryland Supreme Court as stated in the Amended Complaint.

What I reject about elective politics is that after there was peaceful tranquility and no controversy in private, the politicians and media seek majority vs. minority differences in public as a means to create controversy for profiteering by pandering to the various and vicarious interests for votes from others to gain or remain in office, and then they want to project a public image when a spurious image can lead to prejudiced and personal attacks against one another rather than respecting related families and non-personal policies that improves peaceful relations among related families.

A politician is at the whim of the majority that can lead to changing his or her identity and personality into an image of what the majority wants when that can be considered as a spurious mindless fraud wasting religious liberty and independent creativity. Moreover, in elective politics for every winner there are one or more losers, and then when the people are only driven by winners and losers then the result is that there are people uncared for, stigmatized, humiliated, or killed. A politician needs to win the majority against the minority to win, when the Chief Justice is not concerned about winning the majority because he is more concerned about preventing the majority from harming the minority. When the U.S. President speaks of war at the State of Union the U.S. Supreme Court justices opposing expression is because the U.S. Supreme

Court justices are more concerned about humanity. I would rather be friendly with everyone rather than kill anyone therefore I would rather be the Chief Justice. The only way to prevent the majority from harming the minority is by respecting privacy against the mindless that are only driven by popular public opinion that only respect winners while those that are unskilled and unskillful can resort to unethical means such as lying, spying, and disrupting preparations while attempting to defame the character of another, and then projecting unrelated images and fraudulent identities, and is one of the reasons why the U.S. Supreme Court rules for privacy, and then when privacy is invaded a Civil lawsuit can be filled against those that invade privacy and attempt to defame another's character.

After my youngest daughter painted from hope, happiness, a garden, and love, and signatures from sons, father embraced sons then guided sons outside while father closed the door then she placed both arms

on my shoulders and I held her close, and while that

proves her love, others belatedly questioned my love,

when the best of what I can describe of my love was

already written about a night that I resisted, relented,

and discovered a place of eternal love, then after others

invaded privacy and disrupted the loving relationship, I

intimately wrote what I could about that evening then

sent that to my daughter when only words will never

describe that evening while her jealous mother

betrayed and presumptuously took that writing then

sent my writing to the totalitarian terrorists of mob-rule

known as the gestapo in Statesville, N.C. when under

American law the gestapo had to give that writing to my

lawyer whom stated that writing was prolific while later

described that father and daughter were lovers, and

while the motto of where I live is "Virginia is for lovers",

there was more involved when I was also caring for my

sons, then when my lawyer knew the majority would support lovers he awoke the public while disregarding the sanctity of her virginity that should not involve awaking the public when the public would only publically debauch her then play political games while gambling on life, religious liberty, or poetic and art forms with a crowd of intruders while profiteering by insincerely and vicariously entertaining others.

If there was a potent single male living with a fertile single female and after she expressed poetic form and gave her significant other poetic form, then she was satisfied and sincerely promised before visiting others, and then after visiting others she smeared him, then that male would state she is wrong, and if I declare "men are created equal" - Declaration of Independence, 1776, then every "self-evident", supra, man would state she is wrong. I do not believe when Thomas Jefferson wrote "life, liberty, and the pursuit of happiness", supra, that he meant for intruders to recklessly persecute, then hopelessly, heartlessly, and hatefully disrupt another's life, liberty, and happiness. The worse part about others belated and animalistic invasions of privacy is intruders only considered physicality when their invasions are with no cerebral computation, personal obligation, nor respect for "unalienable rights", <u>supra</u>.

A biological father can inculcate from the religion of his choice through the free exercise of religion from his interpretations and his reforms. For example, when some religions forbid drinking and dancing, a biological father can overrule that religion for his family while another father can forbid drinking and dancing when their different connections and beliefs are respectfully separated by different bloodlines, marriages, or private property. The foregoing is what happened when my eldest daughter returned from Church one day and told me I could not go out and dance, and then I overruled her and the Church she was attending, then told her she needs to attend another Church. In North Carolina there are what is referred to as dry Counties that prohibit the sale of alcohol, and while most laws originate from the Bible those that create and enforce public policies must remain neutral rather than "teaching in a school affiliated with his or her faith and operated to inculcate its tenets ... [with] great difficulty in remaining religiously neutral". - <u>Lemon vs. Kurtzman</u>, 403 U.S. 602, 618 (1971).

When incarcerated I sent legal work to my last lawyer, and the last day he (*Matthew Benton*) visited he stated that I was right when I already instinctively knew I was right before the gestapo made "an attempt to coerce ... into capitulating to congressional demands" - <u>United States v. Sioux Nation of Indians</u>, 448 U.S. 371, 419 (1980), as if congress is a father's children collecting votes among one another and then attempting to overrule their father's decision when many fathers will at times consider and accept unanimous votes from his children rather than a majority of vote counts that disregard care for any of his children while at other times a father will put his foot down with an executive privilege and not consider vote counts, especially when his children are immature, or unsuccessful, or unreasonable, or unsentimental, or inconsiderate, or disrespectful. The foregoing was how private families were raised when I grew up. The way a private family works is not the way Democracy works since there is no majority override of their father's veto while I do not appreciate those whom presumptuously and pretentiously make comparisons as if a family is a Democracy. I believe that their belief is from excessive unmerited dysfunctional fatherless families in the last generation that are overexposed to politics and unethical media that disrupt, corrupt, and profligate others, and then follow socialistic policies.

If others continue invading privacy while trying to belatedly take credit after parsing hearsay or my words, then again, they are lucky I did not kill others a decade ago when the words I publish will substantiate my instincts of immediately killing the intruders while others should not expect that my charity should be expected from everyone when if others continue with the status quo then I expect that if there is an adverse ruling against me in the highest Court then if another finds himself in a similar position and situation in the future he should immediately execute the intruders and put an end to others controversial and inconsequential games of no significance. I think about it like this, others have already wasted half the time that would be spent after a murder conviction and that is if there was a murder conviction therefore why would a father subject himself to others incompetence sans justice for half that time rather than seek vigilante justice then relax regardless of others unrelated, inexperience and belated opinion. The foregoing are what some men on the inner-city streets think about Democracy before they kill another.

After critics excessively evaluate then that can lead to eugenics programs from Democracies of the past when if critics continually invade privacy, then a shoe can be put on the other foot, when eugenics programs from Democracies of the past would cull if inferior intellects were discovered while I proved my intellect containing published computations in my first filing in Federal District Court that only high intellects can compute and understand while I discovered many inferior intellects that opposed my lawsuit. The critics should have been focused on what I was critically focused on in the aftermath after others extraneously interfered and excessively entangled when the only substantiation of their frivolous objection is if the next man married her, when he only took her virginity and they did not marry nor are they still together, nor did every one of my children graduate college in their mother's custody while the controversial and inconsequential games of others only foolishly wasted time and money, and are of no significance while future intrusions of another successful family could result in immediate and fatal consequences against the intruders. When a father had advanced his profession while maintaining tranquility in his family with success for every one of his children and then when socialistic degenerates belatedly disrupt thereof, and then if a justice of the peace through the U.S. First Amendment does not support the foregoing tranquility and success, then that is when the Second Amendment of the U.S. Constitution needs to be considered.

After men only want to play games and compete against one another over different ideologies while others bet against one or the other, they are wasting time when I can support inside from a sired gender balance and merited functional family, or outside from a five million women surplus. The miscalculations with many Greeks from votes are misinterpreted as science while the foregoing individuals were already countered by the Romans with census gender counts. The belated voters have only led to genocide rather than peaceful considerations with respect for religion from Moses with the Ten Commandments and virginity with Romans considering census gender counts, and real time psychoanalysis with respect for the neurological scientist turned psychologist Sigmund Freud, and poetic and art forms with respect for Shakespeare, and while I wrote a psychoanalytical perspective, I also wrote from a philosophical perspective about volatile nature while others belated invasion coerces and forces an insincere psychological displacement when their mother should have been put in jail for her involvement in perjury. When a father has multiple reasons for executing the intruders he should not let others get away with attempting to defame a father with their lame, frivolous, and flimsy excuse from vulgar commoners disrespecting genius, progeny, precocious, and prodigy using only three frivolous months before an age that the vulgar commoners accept when the vulgar commoners are not considering precocious, successful, reasonable, respectful, considerate, sensible, sensitive, nor are others true and correct, and then when vulgar commoners want to seek out barbarous words then they will be opposed from: 1: A sired gender balance. 2. Merited functional family. 3. Poetic form. 4. Sincere promise. 5. Art form. ☺. 6. Signatures from sons. 7.

Their father's approval of a healthy, happy, successful, peaceful, and suitable family structure.

What is concerning about the U.S. President, religion, and politics is that his step-brother Mark Obama from Kenya questioned the authority of an Athenian Democracy after Barrack did not show adequate respect for their father by acknowledging their lineage from their father, when under their father and the Declaration of Independence Mark and Barrack were created equal. At the Democratic National Convention Barrack Obama only talked about his family in Kansas because he has been educated by many Greeks to neglect his lineage, oppose their religion, and follow his mother rather than his father while many sons in that situation either work for an Athenian Government or do not want to move away from his mother while every girlfriend he had states he is a momma's boy and then leaves. When Abraham sired two sons with two different women, in religion that would be his two sons regardless of how many women involved while many Greeks would enslave Abraham and then replace Abraham's religion with secular authority and then state each son was from his mother, and then state Abraham was from his mother. In an Athenian Democracy, Abraham would have been subjugated to the pay the State to pay the mother(s) of his two sons. Many Greeks influenced the New Testament by changing the lineage whereas the Old Testament is from father and son, and then a myth was created when stating that while a woman named Mary was relatedly Jewish then therefore Jesus was Jewish after eliminating the biological father with an unscientific and impossible conception when stating there was no D.N.A. from their biological father when their myth changes Adam and Eve to Mary and Jesus while their myth continues in a socialistic welfare-state that only considers the biological father if he has money and then if he has more earnings than the average family income, then they plunder the additional earnings that exceed the average family income when child support that is compelled should not exceed the amount paid by average family incomes. There are modern American women that seduce wealthy men to have his children and then go to D.S.S. to plunder from him while modern mothers that use a socialistic welfare-state are thieves when many fathers believe that if his children are forcibly taken then that father should not have to pay for his children. What is also concerning is that in most religions there is a man with a woman or a man with multiple women while with secular authority a woman with multiple men is approved. I prefer using the census gender count to make a decision, however, when absolute nature is considered, a father does not need secular authority to raise his family while a mother needs outside secular authority that makes an attempt to control children when secular authority causes more violence when they are belatedly reactive and then left to only retrieve the deceased on the inner-city streets.

There are many issues with the teachings from many Greeks while some of the more violent issues are excessive murder rates after mostly fatherless Cities while Athenian governments think they can supplant a father's authority and then take his children and use them to kill or be killed in war and then give them pieces of metal as a reward while soldiers then have to reconcile their conscience while living the rest of their life in and out of veteran hospitals. When a Country becomes less reliant on their father and more reliant on secular authority then a Country can become a socialistic welfare-state with a socialistic Democratic policy and tyranny of the majority after the Democrats discriminated and then want a larger socialistic government while trying to control families and jobs then take away barter or friendly competition when either or will and can improve one another without causing animosity from extraneous, barbarous, and invidious crowds of intruders. There are major issues with Democratic policies. Instead of the Republicans wanting to forever close the borders or the Democrats wanting to forever open the borders, immigration policies should consider merit or the Gross Domestic Product as the determination of opening or closing the borders. If there is a high Gross Domestic Product then the borders can open, if there is a low Gross Domestic Product then the borders need closed. The Gross Domestic Product should also be considered for tariffs and trade agreements. The media is inadequate when a moderator at the last debate stated that both their policies would increase the national debt and then did not know what Donald Trump meant when he responded from the Gross Domestic Product of which meant policies that increase the Gross Domestic Product would eventually decrease the national debt even if there was a short term increase in national debt while Democratic policies would decrease the Gross Domestic Product and never decrease the national debt. The best way to govern is by connecting policies instead of asking which side of a particular policy or political party does another stand on because a policy can be cause and effect on another policy. At this time, Donald Trump would be the best choice if he stops making personal attacks, then gets elected, and works the policies he mentioned that the Country needs at this time. While I do not absolutely agree with the <u>Roe v. Wade</u> decision that gave rights to only a woman followed by worse decisions by the Court when attempting to turn families over to only "areas" when the foregoing has caused the escalation of violence. As for

Donald Trump, he needs to stay away from the <u>Roe v.</u>

<u>Wade</u> decision or he will lose the popular and general

election because Democracy "slaughters some and

banishes the rest" - *Plato*. After it was recently

discovered the Democratic Party incited violence at the

Republican Rallies then the Governors of every State

need to step up and oppose such malicious behavior

and reject the escalation of violence. In regards to

Russia, the only reason Russia was considered an

enemy is because of the two different types of

Governments, however, different types of governments,

like different religions, can coexist without referring to

the other as an enemy, therefore Donald Trump was

right when he stated that it would be good if both

Countries were friendly with one another rather than

placing more Americans and Russians at risk of war.

Like many that respect friendly competitions such as

athletes, I would rather be friendly with for example

Alexander Ovechkin from Russia rather than discriminate, not because of the money others pay, because of his work ethic. Many years ago, I was interested in the conflict among the Countries, however, when the Countries became friendly I realized that was best for both Countries, and then after Democracy started corrupting Russia with unrestrained businessmen and mobs, Russia is in the process of finding a way to moderate and mitigate unrestrained changes over the last 25 years that has not always been for the better, just like America did throughout American history. Most Americans are more concerned about what is going on in America and not Syria, or any other Country; therefore, candidates need to stop talking about their war machines and ghetto scenes of inhumanity and improve the lives of residents since that is the primary reason for being elected.

A civilization can become more civilized if taught earning with merit and charity rather than gang into mob-rule while coercing oppression and more taxes. What the Country does not need at this time are more socialistic majority policies. I reject the foregoing policies, especially when processes thereof incarcerate for years, force harmful drugs, and deprive substantive due process, *see* Amended Complaint p. 7, rather than real computations when why would someone without real computations want to publically insult another rather than get along with one another. I am not trying to create a Marxist policy, however, after the socialists of Social Services were the Marxists that disrupted Capitalism, then if we are competing over ideologies then I will and can create a better social policy than tyranny of the majority from socialism since I do not appreciate the socialists disrupting more merit from Capitalism than the tyranny of the majority from the socialists that disrupt merited functional families and

Capitalism. I believe I am living under a totalitarian

regime of oppression and injustice after the Fourth

Circuit Court denied me an opportunity to state oral

arguments in Court while stating that there was no

irreversible error by the District Court. The claim for

"injury due to negligence" - Black's Law Dictionary, and

5:15-cv-00083-RLV-DCK, [Doc. 30 & 35], misconduct

and conspiracy with coercive obstruction of justice from

Defendant Wall and I.C.N.C.D.S.S with Defendant

Butler, and other lower court errors are as follows:

Rather than "Defendant Wall directed the

Department to take the Plaintiff's four children into

temporary custody", Appx I at 4, it was only my

youngest three while my eldest was assisting her

father; rather than "Defendant Butler threatened his

counsel with charges of obstruction of justice", Id.at 50

& 51, it was Defendant Butler whom coercively

obstructed justice moments before a custody hearing when he threatening charges against Plaintiff if Plaintiff participated in the hearing; rather than "Plaintiff *did* participate in the hearing", Id at 52, I was not seated at counsel's table, I was in the audience where the spectators must remain silent in Court; rather than "last alleges ... on June 5, 2004", Appx II at 11, and "June 5, 2004 and before", Id at 12, it was after June 5th 2004. Then on August 27, 2015, on the day the Motion for Default Judgement under rule 55 (b) (1) of Fed. R. Civ. Pro. was filed in District Court, I received the following email from my youngest daughter whom I had not directly communicated with in the prior ten years.

Hey there Dad, I was trying to find a picture of you on the Internet and came across your LinkedIn page where I found your email address. It's been a very long time since we have spoken, and I'm not sure if this (your) email even works so I'll keep it short until you reply.

Hope to talk to you soon and I hope you are doing well.

Love always, Your Daughter Michelle

The degenerates that belatedly pandered and gossiped with one another were more interested in how long intimacy lasted rather than several years of relative relations, care, and merits. *See:* 5:15-cv-00083-RLV-DCK, [Doc. 18]. Closeness should not be an issue after a sired gender balance and merited functional family against unmerited dysfunctional fatherless families and an imbalanced census gender count with a socialistic welfare-state and tyranny of the majority from the mindless that belatedly discriminated, degenerated, and substantially harmed with no significant benefits against a father providing significant benefits with harmless achievements that were privately and peaceably assembled under the U.S. Fourteenth, Fourth, and First Amendments. In regards to statute of limitation arguments that are not in 42 U.S.C. §§ 1983, 1985,

reparations for African Americans and the Indians were

awarded several decades after a grievance. In regards

to whom was served, only the individuals that

participated and caused the initial and continuous injury

with claim thereof were included and served the

Amended Complaint. Since there was not a current

employee of I.C.N.C.D.S.S. named on the Amended

Complaint, then there is no claim against the current

Director nor claim against the Mayor of the City of

Statesville when they did not participate nor make any

of the injurious decisions, however, the foregoing

entities were made aware of this Civil Action by the

District Court judge, Appx I at 74 & 75, while the City

should have had liability insurance to cover their liability

from their representatives during the time of injury. In

regards to the District Court Judge belatedly requesting

a second Amended Complaint, and then when

considering that the U.S. Supreme Court permits only

three months to respond to a judgment, then the

Defendant should not be permitted more than three

months to respond after a default, especially when the

Plaintiff was at one time a Defendant where the

prosecutor from tyranny of the majority threatened the

Defendant with charges and then the Defendant

responded within three months with a religious patristic

writing and then the prosecutor charged the Defendant

and then played confidence games, then the Defendant

became Plaintiff and filed a Civil Action against the

prosecutor then after prosecutor as Defendant did not

respond within three months, the Defendant defaulted.

In regards to rule 55 (b) (1) of Fed. R. Civ. Pro., the

Federal District judge wrote many pages in his first

Order, Appx I, in his attempt to arbitrarily overrule rules

of civil procedure when if there are contingencies with

that rule then every contingency, of which I believe I

surpassed, should have been published in that rule as to not mislead and substantially burden pro se plaintiffs that spent most of their life in another profession that are more capitalistic than socialistic, then compelled to study CASELAW for as many years as the Federal judge to determine if a rule of civil procedure that the defendant failed to follow could be arbitrarily dismissed by a District Court judge when relying on tyranny of the majority from lower courts. The foregoing is what also happened in July 2004 in the State District Court of Dundalk, Md, when their mother's boyfriend arbitrarily dismissed rules of civil procedure. *See*: 5:15-cv-00083-RLV-DCK, [Doc. 19], and Appx. III at 25, 27. When there are no rules of civil procedure then there is only violence when I thought about the Second Amendment of the U.S Constitution in July 2004 and then decided to give the U.S. Justice System an opportunity while thus far the U.S. Justice System has failed the Fourteenth,

Fourth, and First Amendments of the U.S. Constitution

leaving only the Second Amendment of the U.S.

Constitution that I now staunchly support, and while the

foregoing might seem to advocate more violence, the

foregoing consideration was only after a real grievance

was denied when that grief also included the last social

worker that previously observed me interacting with my

sons and discovered, like my last wife, that I was a

good father while my last wife returned in Court with me

and observed the slanderous custody hearing where

the last social worker was overruled by Defendant Wall

conspiring with Defendant Butler, and then after I

opened the doors of Court and witnessed the last social

worker grieving after she had previously discovered the

malicious intent of I.C.N.C.D.S.S that wanted children

slandering their father, and while I was unaware of

others malicious intent, and then heard slander under

oath, I grieved, followed by a religious patristic writing.

CONCLUSION

From the facts, legal contentions, and the
foregoing statements of the case, the petitioner
requests the United States Supreme Court reverse the
October 17, 2016 judgment from the Federal Fourth
Circuit Court against the Petitioner and reinstate the
First Amended Complaint filed in the Federal District
Court with the default judgment, or return this case with
corrections to the Federal District or the Federal Circuit
Court for filings, or oral arguments.

This the _____ day of November 2016.

BY: _____
David Thomas Silvers Sr.

APPENDIX I

IN THE UNITED STATES DISTRICT COURT

FOR THE WESTERN DISTRICT OF NORTH CAROLINA

STATESVILLE DIVISION

CIVIL ACTION NO. 5:15-CV-00083-RLV-DCK

DAVID THOMAS SILVERS, SR.,   )

    Plaintiff,   )

    v.   )   **ORDER**

IREDELL COUNTY DEPARTMENT)

OF SOCIAL SERVICES; D.S.S. DIR)

DONALD C. WALL, IN HIS   )

INDIVIDUAL AND OFFICIAL   )

CAPACITIES; ASST. D.A. PAXTON)

BUTLER, IN HIS INDIVIDUAL AND)

OFFICIAL CAPACITIES, AND THE)

CITY OF STATESVILLE, N.C.,   )

    Defendants.   )

_____)

THIS MATTER IS BEFORE THE COURT on

Plaintiff's Motion for Default Judgment (Doc. No. 16)

and Defendants' Motion to Dismiss Plaintiff's First

Amended Complaint as to Defendants Iredell County

Department of Social Services (the "Department") and

Donald C. Wall (Doc. No. 5).[1] Because the parties'

submissions are filed and pending, this matter is ripe for

the Court's review. After a thorough review of the

record, the Court **DENIES** Plaintiff's Motion for Default

Judgement and **DENIES WITHOUT PREJUDICE**

---

[1] While the motion to dismiss purports to have been only brought by Defendant Wall, the motion states, on its face, that it has been brought by Defendant Wall in his "individual and official" capacities. [Doc. No. 5] at p. 1. And official capacity claim is, in actuality, a claim against the government entity employing the individual named in the lawsuit. See, e.g., Graham v. Kentucky, 473 U.S. 159, 165-66 (1985) ("Official-capacity suits, in contrast, generally represent only another way of pleading an action against an entity of which an officer is an agent. As long as the government entity receives notice and an opportunity to respond, an official-capacity suit is, in all respects other than name, to be treated as a suit against the entity." (internal quotations and citations omitted)). Because Defendant Wall has filed the motion to dismiss in his individual and official capacities, the Court will treat the motion as having been filed by both Defendant Wall, individually, and the Department. See Graham, 473 U.S. at 165-166.

Defendants' Motion to Dismiss. Plaintiff is **GRANTED
LEAVE** to file a second amended complaint, as
provided below.

I. BACKGROUND

A. Factual Allegations

Plaintiff David T. Silvers, Sr. is the father of four
children – two boys and two girls. [Doc, No, 2] at ¶ 1. In
December 2000, Plaintiff had retained custody of his
eldest child and was pursuing custody of his three
younger children. Id. On December 26, 2000, Plaintiff
was awarded custody of his three younger children by a
Maryland state court. Id. On April 21, 2003, Plaintiff's
award of custody was affirmed by a Maryland appellate
court. Id. at ¶ 2. At that time, the four children were
residing with Plaintiff at a residence located in
Statesville, North Carolina. Id.

On June 5, 2004, Plaintiff's three youngest
children visited their mother for the summer. [Doc. No.

2] at ¶ 3. At some point thereafter, Defendant Wall directed the Department to take the Plaintiff's four children into temporary custody. Id. A guardian ad litem was also appointed for the children. Id. While they were in the temporary custody of the Department, the Plaintiff was permitted to have only supervised visits with the children. Id. Plaintiff claims that his "freedom of speech was suppressed [during his supervised visits] by social workers" acting under Defendant Wall's orders. Id. The children's mother, however, was permitted to visit the children unsupervised. Id. During these visits, Plaintiff claims that the mother "continued coercing;" yet, Plaintiff does not allege who was coerced, how such person(s) were coerced, or for what purpose such person(s) were "coerced." Id. Sometime between June 2004 and March 2005, a custody hearing was scheduled. [Doc. No. 2] at ¶¶ 3-4. While the Plaintiff's children were in temporary custody, the Department allegedly "conspired with [the] Assistant District Attorney of Iredell County" Paxton Butler – through the First Amended Complaint does not specify the substance of the alleged "conspiracy" or its purpose. Id. at ¶ 3. Defendant Butler threatened Plaintiff's counsel with criminal charges related to obstruction of justice "if [Plaintiff] proceeded with [the] custody hearing ..." Id. During the custody hearing, "there was slander from hearsay" by a social worker, and custody was "prejudicially and illegitimately taken" from Plaintiff and awarded to the mother "Iredell County and the City of Statesville."[1] Id.

---

[1] "Iredell County" has not been named as a party to this lawsuit. Rather, as far as the Court can divine, the only county entity against which claims have been made is the Department. Plaintiff's claim against Defendant Butler in his "official capacity" is not a claim against Iredell County because, under North Carolina law, Defendant Butler is not an employee of the county; rather, he is an official employee of the State of North Carolina. See N.C. Const. art. IV, §§ 18, 20; accord N.C. Gen. Stat. §§ 7A-60, 7A-65; see also McNair v. Nash County, 2012 U.S. Dist. LEXIS 99614, at *5-6 (E.D.N.C. 2012).

On March 11, 2005, Defendant Butler "maliciously, insensibly and needlessly" filed "spurious and totalitarian charges" of "indecent liberties" and "statutory rape" against the Plaintiff by utilizing "what he wanted from the correspondence between [Plaintiff] and [the] Ad Litem[,] while disregarding the exculpatory claim ... [that] there was libelous slander from [P]laintiff's sired children [that was] coerced by the mother." Id. at ¶ 5. Plaintiff claims that, by omitting exculpatory evidence from his presentation, Defendant Butler "mislead" the grand jury. Id. The only "exculpatory evidence" allegedly not disclosed by Defendant Butler was "[Plaintiff's] claim[] that the mother, with no credibility, coerced [Plaintiff's] sired children into slandering their father[.]" Id. Plaintiff does allege that, on November 25, 2014, these "charges" were expunged by order of a state court in Iredell County. Id. at ¶ 9.

Plaintiff alleges that he protested Defendant Butler's action on September 19, 2007. Id. at ¶ 6. On October 12, 2007, Defendant Butler charged Plaintiff with "fraudulently burning [a] dwelling." Id. Defendant claims that this charge was unlawful because "higher State Courts previously held that charge does not apply" when neither substantial harm to another nor insurance fraud results from the act. Id. Plaintiff does not allege whether he was convicted of this charge plead this charge, or whether this charge was dropped.

On January 25, 2009, Plaintiff was confined to prison or was otherwise taken into the custody of the state; however, the First Amended Complaint does not allege whether the detention resulted from any of the above-mentioned charges, whether it occurred as the result of a trial or plea, or whether it resulted from some sort of civil detention or guardianship. Id. at ¶ 7. In fact, the First Amended Complaint does not allege *why*

Defendant was taken into custody in 2009 or *who* initiated and directed the legal process against the Plaintiff. While confined by the state, Plaintiff was "deprived of liberty and due process" because he was improperly sent to a "state mental institution," which allegedly forced him to take "harmful drugs." Id. Plaintiff does not allege *who* improperly sent him "back and forth" to this "mental institution" or *who* forced him to take "harmful drugs." Plaintiff was released from custody on August 28, 2012 because of a "dismissal" Id.

B. Procedural Background

On June 30, 2015, Plaintiff filed his Complaint in this Court against the above-named defendants. [Doc. No. 1]. On July 21, 2015, Plaintiff filed his First Amended Complaint. [Doc. No. 2]. Plaintiff has brought his claims pursuant to Sections 1983 and 1985 of Title 42 of the United States Code. Id. On July 22, 2015,

Defendant Wall was personally served with summons and the First Amended Complaint. [Doc. No. 4]. On July 27th, 2015, Defendant Butler was personally served with summons and the First Amended Complaint. [Doc. No. 10]. The City of Statesville (the "City") has never been served – despite Plaintiff making certain accusations that can be construed to include the City. See Fed. R. Civ. Pro. 4(j) (2). Further, Iredell County has never been served – despite Plaintiff alleging an "official capacity" claim against Defendant Butler, a state employee. Id.

On July 30, 2015, Defendant Wall and the Department filed a motion to dismiss, which is currently pending before the Court. [Doc. No. 5]. Defendant Butler has never plead or otherwise defended against Plaintiff's First Amended Complaint. On August 21, 2015, Plaintiff filed a motion for entry of default against Defendant Butler, which was entered on August 24, 2015. [Doc. No. 14]; [Doc. No. 15]. On August 27, 2015, the plaintiff filed a motion for default judgment against Defendant Butler. [Doc. No. 16].

II. DISCUSSION

A. Plaintiff's Motion for Default Judgment against Defendant Butler

1. Legal Standard of Review Applicable to Motion for Default Judgment

Plaintiff's motion for default judgement is governed by Rule 55 of the Federal Rules of Civil Procedure. Fed. R. Civ. Pro. 55. Upon showing that a party against whom judgment is sought has failed to plead or otherwise defend, the clerk must enter the party's default, Fed. R. Civ. P. 55 (a). After the clerk has entered a default, the plaintiff may seek a default judgment. See Fed. R. Civ. P. 55(b). The entry of a default judgment is left to the sound discretion of the court and no party is entitled to a favorable entry of default judgment as a matter of right. See Black v. F &

S, LLC, 2008 U.S. Dist. LEXIS 100577, at *6 n.6

(W.D.N.C. 2008) (Voorhees, J.) (citing United States v.

Ragin, 113 F.3d 1233, 1997 U.S. App. LEXIS 11827, at

*5 (4th Cir.1997)); Draper vs. Coombs, 792 F.2d 915,

924 (9th Cir. 1986)) see also Advantage Media Group

v. Debnam, 2011 U.S. Dist. LEXIS 62678, at *3

(M.D.N.C. 2011); EMI April Music, Inc. v. White, 618 F.

Supp. 2d 497, 505 (E.D. Va 2009); S.E.C. v. Lawbaugh,

395 F. Supp. 2d 418, 421 (D. Md. 2005). Without

question, because the American civil litigation system is

adversarial by nature, it is the "strong policy" of the

Fourth Circuit to decide cases on the merits. See, e.g.,

Colleton Prep. Academy, Inc. v. Hoover Universal, Inc.,

616 F.3d 413, 417-21 (4th Cir. 2010). However, default

judgment serves as an appropriate remedy in certain

circumstances where the adversarial system breaks

down. See Dow Corning Corp. v. Xiao, 2013 U.S. Dist.

LEXIS 11096, at *8-9 (E.D. Mich. 2013). A breakdown

typically occurs where a party, against whom affirmative

relief is sought, refuses to engage in adversarial

litigation. Id.

Per Rule 55(b), the well-pleaded factual

allegations of the complaint that concern liability are

deemed admitted upon a party's default, in contrast to

allegations concerning only damages or conclusions of

law. See Cannon v. Exum, 1986 U.S. App. LEXIS

38066, at *8 (4th Cir. 1987) (citing Nishimatsu Constr.

Co. v. Houston National Bank, 515 F.2d 1200, 1206

(5th Cir. 1975)); see also Dundee Cement Co. v.

Howard Pipe & Concrete Prods., 722 F.2d 1319, 1323

(7th Cir. 1983); accord Fed. R. Civ. P. 8(b) (6) (a

defaulting party is deemed to admit factual allegations

of the plaintiff's complaint, "other than [those] relating to

the amount of damages"). Although a defaulting party

"admits the plaintiff's well-pleaded allegations of fact" as to liability, the party in default is "not held ... to admit conclusions of law" or allegations regarding liability that are not "well-pleaded." Ryan v. Homecomings Fin. Network, 253 F.3d 778, 780 (4th Cir. 2001). Thus, "a default is not treated as an absolute confession by the defendant of his liability and of the plaintiff's right to recover." Id. (citation omitted); see also 10A WRIGHT, MILLER & CANE, FED. PRAC & PROC. CIV., § 2688 (3d ed. 1998) ("WRIGHT, MILLER") ([L]iability is not deemed established simply because of the default, and the court, in its discretion, may require some proof of the facts that must be established in order to determine liability.") accord Ohio Cent R. Co. v. Central Trust Co., 133 U.S. 83, 91 (1890).

A plaintiff's burden in moving for default judgment is not satisfied, however, by simply pleading facts; rather, the plaintiff's complaint must also state a cognizable claim to which his or her well-pleaded facts provide support and show an entitlement to relief. See Ryan, 253 F.3d at 780 "The court must, therefore, determine whether the well-pleaded allegations in [the plaintiff's] complaint support the relief sought ..."); 10A WRIGHT, MILLER, § 2688 ("[I]t remains for the court to consider whether the unchallenged facts constitute a legitimate cause of action ..."). Indeed, "[a] default judgment is unassailable on the merits ... only so far as it is supported by *well-pleaded* allegations, assumed to be true." Nishimatsu, 515 F.2d. at 1206 (citing Thomson v. Wooster, 114 U.S. 104 (1885)) (emphasis in original).

In Nishimatsu, *supra*, a leading default judgment case, the Fifth Circuit, reviewed a situation wherein default was awarded for breach of contract under Texas law. There, an individual named Jack Baize signed a contract on behalf of South East Construction Company ("SECON"). Id at 1205. The contract was allegedly breached and Nishimatsu sued Baize individually for

the breach – obtaining a default judgment against him.
Id. The Fifth Circuit reversed. The court observed that
Baize had signed the contract by writing SECON's
name, followed by "By: Jack D. Baize." Id. at 1205.
According to the Fifth Circuit, Nishimatsu's complaint
alleged that both Baize and SECON were parties to the
contract; however, the court noted that this allegation
was "contradicted and controlled by the contract
showing that Baize signed only as an agent." Id. at
1206. Applying Texas law, the court reasoned that, "if
an agent signs a contract for a disclosed principal, he
does not intend to make himself a party to the
instrument," and the signature form used by Baize was
"uniformly regarded as indicating that the principal
alone and not the agent is a party to the contract." Id. at
1207. For this reason, the court concluded that the
contract "binds only [SECON]. [Thus,] [t]he complaint,
to the extent that it seeks relief against Baize on that

contract, is incapable of supporting the default judgment." Id. at 1208. Specifically, the court found that the complaint did not allege a "sufficient basis" to support the default judgment against Baize. Id. at 1206.

The Fourth Circuit has relied on Nishimatsu in crafting its interpretation of Rule 55(b) and in pronouncing the standard that district courts should apply when reviewing a motion for default judgment. See, e.g., Ryan, 253 F.3d at 780; see also DirecTV, Inc. v Pernites, 200 Fed. App'x 257, 258 (4th Cir. 2006). Interpreting Rule 55 and Nishimatsu, the Fourth Circuit has declared that, upon a plaintiff's application for default judgment, district courts have an obligation to review the complaint to determine whether the plaintiff has alleged well-pleaded facts and, assuming those well-pleaded facts are true, whether the complaint states a "sufficient basis" on which judgment may be entered. Ryan, 253 F.3d at 780 ("The defendant, by his default, admits the plaintiff's well-pleaded allegations of fact" so a court must "determine whether the well-pleaded allegations of fact" so a court must "determine whether the well-pleaded allegations in [the] complaint support the relief sought in th[e] action." (quoting and relying on Nishimatsu, 515 F.2d at 1206); see also DirecTV, 200 Fed. App'x at 258 ("[A] defendant's default does not itself warrant the court in entering a default judgment. There must be a "sufficient basis" in the pleadings for the judgment entered." (quoting Nishimatsu, 515 F.2d at 1206) (alteration in original)); accord Balt. Line Handling Co. v. Brophy, 771 F.Supp 2d 531, 540-47 (D. Md. 2011). However, the Fourth Circuit has not elaborated on what Nishimatsu's "sufficient basis" requirement means. See DirecTV, Inc., 200 Fed. App'x at 258; Balt. Line Handling Co., 771 F.Supp. 2d at 544.

Recently, other circuits have weighed in and have

read Nishimatsu to require the application of a hybrid

motion to dismiss standard in the default judgment

context. See Surtain v. Hamlin Terrace Found., 789

F.3d 1239, 1244-45 (11th Cir. June 16, 2015); Wooten

v. McDonald Transit Assocs., Inc., 788 F.3d 490, 496

(5th Cir. June 10, 2015). Interpreting Nishimatsu, the

Eleventh Circuit determined that it is appropriate to

apply the Rule 12(b)(6) standard announced in the

Supreme Court's Twombly and Iqbal decisions to

motions for default judgment, stating that "[a]lthough

Nishimatsu did not elaborate as to what constitutes 'a

sufficient basis' for the [default] judgment, we have

subsequently interpreted the standard as being akin to

that necessary to survive a motion to dismiss for failure

to state a claim"); see also Ashcroft v. Iqbal, 556 U.S.

662 (2009); Bell Atl. Corp v. Twombly, 550 U.S. 544

(2007). So holding, the Eleventh Circuit determined that

"a motion for default judgment is like a reverse motion to dismiss for failure to state a claim." Surtain, 789 F.3d at 1245.

The Fifth Circuit, however, recently vacated a decision that announced a standard similar to the one adopted by the Eleventh Circuit. Compare Wooten v McDonald Transit Assocs., Inc., 788 F.3d 490, 496-500 (5th Cir. Jan. 2, 2015) with Wooten v. McDonald Transit Assocs., 775 F.3d 689, 695-96 (5th Cir. Jan. 2, 2015). In its opinion, the court opted for an amorphous, less-strict standard, which, nevertheless, finds its basis in the same Supreme Court decisions. See Wooten, 788 F.3d at 496-500 (declining to apply the strict Rule 12(b)(6) standard announced in Twombly and Iqbal, thus vacating the previous panel decision, but adopting a less-strict standard that requires "more than an unadorned, the-defendant-unlawfully-harmed-me accusation" (citing Iqbal, 556 U.S. at 678)). The Fifth

Circuit grounded its reasoning in a distinction between a motion to dismiss under Rule 12(b)(6) and a motion for default judgment under Rule 55. Id. at 498 n.3. The court held that because a defendant must ordinarily "invoke Rule 12" to "avail itself of that rule's protections[,]" it is inappropriate to apply a strict Twombly and Iqbal standard to a motion for default judgment because such a notion "is the product of a defendant's inaction[.]" Id. (emphasis in original).

The Fourth Circuit has not yet announced an opinion that explicitly applies either the Twombly/Iqbal standard or a similar, yet less demanding, standard in the default judgment context. See Balt. Line Handling, 771 F.Supp 2d at 544. However, other district courts in this Circuit have utilized the Twombly/Iqbal standard in such context. See e.g., Russell v. Railey, 2012 U.S. Dist. LEXIS 49370, at *7-8 (D. Md. 2012); Balt. Line Handling, 771 F.Supp. at 544; Wynne v. Birach, 2009

U.S. Dist. LEXIS 102276, at *6 n.6 (E.D. Va 2009)(default judgment standard is "similar to that applied to a motion to dismiss" under Iqbal); Bogopa Serv. Corp. v. Shulga, 2009 U.S. Dist. LEXIS 48469, at *3-4 (W.D.N.C. 2009)(Reidinger, J.)("While in the context of a motion for default judgment the Court is not determining whether a claim has been stated upon which relief can be granted, but rather is determining whether to grant relief based on the presumed truth of the allegations, the standard of legal analysis is the same: can relief be granted based on the allegations made?").

This Court is persuaded that Twombly and Iqbal govern its review of the Plaintiff's motion for default judgment. The Court reaches this conclusion because it is not persuaded by the Fifth Circuit's reasoning for applying a less-strict standard. The Fifth Circuit declined to strictly apply Twombly and Iqbal because a motion to dismiss requires action from a defendant, while a motion for default judgment does not. However, this Court finds that the Fifth Circuit's distinction relies on form over substance.

In general, a plaintiff may seek relief only if the plaintiff has sustained a harm, which may be articulated into a plausible claim for relief that is buttressed with well-plead factual support. Compare Fed. R. Civ. Pro. 8(a); Iqbal, 556 U.S. at 678; Twombly, 550 U.S. at 570. A plaintiff carries the burden of stating his claim and proving that he is entitled to the relief sought – from the commencement of the action through its termination. The Fifth Circuit's opinion fails to recognize or discuss this burden, particularly as it applies when a plaintiff seeks affirmative relief from the court by way of a motion. While the Fifth Circuit correctly points out that Rule 12 and Rule 55 motions are procedurally different, the opinion assumes that this procedural difference is determinative without discussing *how* it is determinative

or *how* it affects a plaintiff's ultimate burden to prove

that he is entitled to the affirmative, substantive relief

sought. Remarkably, in making its distinction between

Rule 12 and Rule 55 motions, the court seems to imply

that, because the "failure to state a claim" defense was

not raised by a defendant at the pleading stage, the

plaintiff is somehow released from his or her burden to

state a claim. Wooten, 788 F.3d at 498 n.3 (implying

that a plaintiff's burden to state a claim must be

"invoke[d]" under Rule 12 before that "rule's

protections" may apply). However, one need only look

to the Rules themselves to see that this is not the case.

See Fed. R. Civ. Por. 8(c)(1)("failure to state a claim" is

not an affirmative defense that is waived by failing to

plead); Fed. R. Civ. Pro. 12(h)(1)&(2)("failure to state a

claim" is not waived by omission from a motion or

pleading, and may be raised by later motion or at trial).

This apparent failure in logic undermines the Fifth

Circuit's reasoning.

While a defendant carries the burden to show that

the plaintiff's complaint should be dismissed under Rule

12(b)(6), the plaintiff *always* carries the burden to prove

that he should be granted affirmative relief on his claims

by way of motion. Hence, a plaintiff carries the burden

of proving that the court should affirmatively grant him

judgment on the pleadings or summary judgment. See,

e.g., Hill v. Terrell, 846 F.Supp. 2d 488, 490 (W.D.N.C.

2012) (Conrad, C.J.) ("A Rule 12(c) motion should only

be granted if the moving party has clearly established

that no material issue of fact remains to be resolved

and the party is entitled to judgment as a matter of law."

(quotation and citations omitted)); Kontane, Inc. v.

Banish, 2011 U.S. Dist. LEXIS 96899, at *5 (W.D.N.C.

2011) (Voorhees. J) (same); see also Kirkman v. Tison,

2012 U.S. Dist. LEXIS 148587, at *24-29 (M.D.N.C.

2012) (discussing and applying standard where plaintiff moves for summary judgment); Great Divide Ins. Co. v. Midnight Rodeo. Inc., 2010 U.S. Dist. LEXIS 51598, at *4-5 (E.D.N.C. 2010) (same). When filing a Rule 55 (b) motion for default judgment, a plaintiff similarly asks the court to grant affirmative relief on his or her claims, as a matter of law, in the form of a judgment based on the factual allegations of the complaint, which are deemed admitted as a result of the defendant's failure to plead. See Fed. R. Civ. Pro. 8(b)(6); Fed. R. Civ. Pro. 55(b)(2). The Court finds that such a request is analogous to a motion for judgment on the pleadings under Rule 12(c), thus a similar legal standard should apply in both contexts. See Perez v. Wells Fargo N.A., 774 F.3d 1329, 1337 (11th Cir. 2014) (recognizing that Rule 55 "dovetails with Rule 12(c).

In the Fourth Circuit, a motion for judgment on the pleadings is analyzed under the same standard as a

Rule 12(b)(6) motion to dismiss. <u>See</u> <u>Independence</u> <u>News, Inc.</u> v. <u>City of Charlotte</u>, 568 F.3d 148, 154 (4th Cir. 2009); <u>Burbach Broad. Co. v. Elkins Radio Corp.</u>, 278 F.3d 401, 405-06 (4th Cir. 2002). Thus, the Fourth Circuit requires that <u>Twombly</u> and <u>Iqbal</u> be applied when reviewing a motion for judgment on the pleadings. <u>See</u> <u>Deutsche Bank Nat'l Trust Co. v. IRS</u>, 361 Fed. App'x 527, 529 (4th Cir. 2010) (citing <u>Monroe v. City of Charlottesville</u>, 579 F.3d 380, 386 (4th Cir. 2009)); <u>accord</u> <u>Fitzhenry v. Indep.Order of Foresters</u>, 2015 U.S. Dist. LEXIS 76750, at *3-4 (D.S.C. 2015); *Mullins v. GMAC Mortg., LLC*, 2011 U.S. Dist. LEXIS 35210, at *4-5 (S.D.W. Va. 2011). Because a Rule 55 motion "dovetails" a Rule 12(c) motion for judgment on the pleadings, this Court, like the Eleventh Circuit, finds that the Rule 12(b)(6) motion to dismiss standard – which includes <u>Twombly</u>, <u>Iqbal</u>, and their progeny – applies to a plaintiff's motion for default judgment.

Accordingly, when reviewing a motion for default judgment, this Court must examine the legal sufficiency of the facts alleged on the face of the plaintiff's complaint. Edwards v. City of Goldsboro, 178 F.3d 231, 243 (4th Cir. 1999); accord Ryan, 253 F.3d at 780. In order to be granted a favorable default judgment, the complaint's "[f]actual allegations must be enough to raise a right to relief above the speculative level." Twombly, 550 U.S. at 555. Indeed, the "complaint must contain sufficient factual matter, accepted as true, to 'state a claim to relief that is plausible on its face.'" Iqbal. 556 U.S. at 678 (quoting Twombly, 550 U.S. at 570). A claim is facially plausible when the factual content allows the court to reasonably infer that the defendant is liable for the misconduct alleged. Id.

When considering a motion for default judgment, the court must accept as true all of the well-plead factual allegations contained in the complaint. See

Erickson v. Pardus, 551 U.S. 89, 94 (2007). However, a pleading that offers mere "labels and conclusions" or "a formulaic recitation of the elements of a cause of action will not do." Iqbal, 556 U.S. at 678. In order to claim relief, the complaint must allege facts that imply more than a "sheer possibility that a defendant has acted unlawfully" or "facts that are 'merely consistent with' a defendant's liability[.]" Id. at 678 (quoting Twombly, 550 U.S. at 557). Critically, "'[t]he presence ... of a few conclusory legal terms does not insulate a complaint from dismissal ... when the facts alleged in the complaint' cannot support the legal conclusion" alleged or relief sought. See Migdal v. Rowe Price-Fleming Int'l, 248 F.3d 321, 326 (4th Cir. 2001) (quoting Young v. City of Mount Ranier, 238 F.3d 567, 577 (4th Cir. 2001)). "Legal inferences drawn from the facts, unwarranted inferences, unreasonable conclusions, or arguments are not part of the consideration." Dolgaleva

v. Va. Beach City Pub, Sch., 364 Fed. App'x 820, 827

(4th Cir. 2010); see also Eastern Shore Mkts., Inc. v.

J.D. Assocs LLP, 213 F.3d 175, 180 (4th Cir. 2000).

In applying this standard, the Supreme Court has

reiterated that '[a] document filed *pro se* is to be

liberally construed and a *pro se* complaint, however

inartfully pleaded, must be held to less stringent

standards than formal pleadings drafted by lawyers."

Erickson, 551 U.S. at 94 (internal citations and

quotation marks omitted); Dolgaleva, 364 Fed. App'x at

827. However, the Fourth Circuit has "not read Erickson

to undermine Trombly's requirement that a pleading

contain more than labels and conclusions[.]" Giarratano

v. Johnson, 521 F.3d 298, 304 n.5 (4th Cir. 2008)

(internal quotation marks omitted (applying Twombly

standard in dismissing *pro se* complaint); accord

Atherton v. Dist. of Columbia Off. Of Mayor, 567 F.3d

672, 681-682 (D.C. Cir. 2009) ("A *pro se* complaint ...

'must be held to less stringent standards than formal pleadings drafted by lawyers.' But even a *pro se* complainant must plead 'factual matter' that permits the court to infer 'more than the mere possibility of misconduct.'" (quoting <u>Erickson</u>, 55 U.S. at 94; <u>Iqbal</u>, 556 U.S. at 679)). The rules governing the generous construction of *pro se* pleadings "do[] not relieve the plaintiff of the burden of alleging sufficient facts on which a recognized legal claim could be based." <u>Ashby v. City of Charlotte</u>, 2015 U.S. Dist. LEXIS 103286 at *4 (W.D.N.C. Aug. 6 2015); <u>Godfrey v. Long</u>, 2012 U.S. Dist. LEXIS 2671, at *3-4 (E.D.N.C. 2012) (quoting <u>Hall v. Bellmon</u>, 935 F.2d 1106, 1110 (10th Cir. 1991)).

2. Issues Presented by the Plaintiff's

Motion for Default Judgment [1]

In his First Amended Complaint, the Plaintiff

makes a variety of opaque and vague allegations,

which have coalesced into an almost indecipherable

conglomeration of labels and legal conclusions, as well

---

[1] The Court notes that, though the majority of Plaintiff's allegations occurred several years ago, Plaintiff's First Amended Complaint cannot be dismissed as to Defendant Butler because of an applicable statute of limitations since, by failing to plead or otherwise defend against the First Amended Complaint, he has currently waived the ability to assert this affirmative defense. See, e.g., United States v. Williams, 684 F.2d 296 (4th Cir. 1982) (Statute of limitations ... is an affirmative defense that may be waived"). United States v. Wild, 551 F.2d 418 (D.C. Cir. 1977) ("Statute of limitations is not a jurisdictional bar, but mere affirmative defense"); See also Vance v. Hedrick, 659 F.2d 447 (4th Cir. 1981) ("Time bars to prosecution or trial of criminal cases, as of civil cases, are affirmative defenses which may be waived.") Likewise, though many of Plaintiff's allegations against Defendant Butler may be subject to the absolute immunity afforded to prosecutors, Defendant Butler has similarly waived this defense by failing to plead in response to the First Amended Complaint. See Owens v. Balt. City State's Attys. Office, 767 F.3d 379, 393 n.4 (4th Cir. 2014). Whether these defenses may be revived if Plaintiff files a second amended complaint is an open question. Compare E.E.O.C. v. Morgan Stanley & Co., Inc., 211 F.R.D. 225, 227 (S.D.N.Y. 2002) (no); Massey v. Helman, 196 F.3d 727, 735 (7th Cir. 2000) (yes); cf DiLoreto v. Oaklyn, 744 F. Supp. 610, 617 (D. N.J. 1990).

as wearisome exposition regarding irrelevant matters. With regard to actual well-pleaded factual matters, there is an utter dearth of material available for the Court to review. For the purpose of analyzing the pending motions, this Court has exerted considerable effort in the hope of untangling Plaintiff's essential claims from the hodgepodge of allegations found in the First Amended Complaint. Based on this evaluation, the Court extrapolates that the Plaintiff alleges the following:

Plaintiff claims that he has been deprived of "security, privacy, liberty, and property without due process of law" and that these deprivations have violated his rights under the "First, Fourth, and Fourteenth Amendments of the United States Constitution" and "International Human Rights." [Doc. No. 2] at p. 1. He claims that his children were placed in foster care and custody was awarded to their mother in violation of his "First, Fourth, and Fourteenth

Amendment[]" rights. [1] [Doc. No. 2] at p. 2 (¶ 2). He

conclusory claims his "freedom of speech" was

suppressed by social worker (on orders of Defendant

Wall) during his supervised visits with his children at the

Department. [2] Id. He also claims that Defendant Butler

improperly threatened his counsel with criminal charges

if Plaintiff contested custody at his children's custody

hearing. Id. Moreover, he claims that his children were

"prejudicially and illegitimately taken" from him during

---

[1] This claim appears to be made only against the Department and Defendant Wall – not Defendant Butler. See footnote 5, *infra*.

[2] Because this claim pertains only to Defendant Wall, in his individual and official capacities the Court will not analyze whether it is sufficient under Twombly and Iqbal. This Order primarily addresses only whether Plaintiff's motion for default judgment should be granted in light of the well-plead allegations of the First Amended Complaint. The Order does not undertake this analysis because, in its discretion, the Court will allow the Plaintiff to file a second amended complaint. This will allow the Plaintiff an opportunity to cure his deficient pleading. Once Plaintiff files his second amended complaint, or if Plaintiff fails to file a second amended complaint, Defendant Wall and/or the Department may re-file the motion to dismiss with respect to the allegations made against them.

the custody hearing by "Iredell County" and the "City of

Statesville" [1] Id. Plaintiff further claims that his "non-

threatening freedom of speech in a religion writing" sent

to his children's guardian ad litem was shared with

Defendant Butler without his consent and Defendant

Butler unlawfully used such correspondence against

him in grand jury proceedings. Id. at 3 (¶ 4). He also

claims that Defendant Butler filed "spurious and

totalitarian charges" of "indecent liberties" and "statutory

rape" against him by misleading a grand jury through

the omission of "significant information that would

negate probably cause," such as Plaintiff's claim that

his children's mother "coerced" the children to "slander"

---

[1] As in the case of the allegations against Defendant Wall and the Department, this Order will not analyze any allegations made against the City or the Iredell County government. Because neither entity has been served with the First Amended Complaint. Plaintiff is not entitled to default judgment (or any other affirmative relief) against such entities. To the extent Plaintiff alleges that the custody determination *itself* violated his constitutional rights, and that such violation is the result of the actions of "Iredell County," through the Department, the Court will not discuss this claim for the reasons specified in footnote 5. *Supra.*

the Plaintiff and to represent that he forced them to live in an "unstable" and "oppressi[ve]" home. Id. at p. 4 (¶ 5). On November 25, 2014, these "charges" were expunged by a state court in Iredell County. Id. at p. 6 (¶ 8).

Plaintiff also appears to claim that he was "harassingly, maliciously, and incompetently deprived of property" when, on October 12, 2007, Defendant Butler charged him with "fraudulently burning [a] dwelling." Id. at p. 5 (¶ 6). However, Plaintiff makes no factual allegation regarding what "property" was taken from him or how such "property" was taken. Plaintiff also appears to allege that Defendant Butler charged him with "fraudulently burning [a] dwelling" in contravention of unspecified state law. Id.

Finally, Plaintiff alleges that he was "deprived of liberty and due process" because, while in state custody between January 2009 through August 2012, he was "improperly" sent "back and forth a few times to a State mental institution," which "forc[ed]" him to take "harmful drugs" after the same mental institution had "cleared" him in October 2007. Id. at p. 6.(¶ 7). Plaintiff does not allege that his actual confinement between 2009 and 2012 was unlawful. Nor does Plaintiff allege who caused him to be sent "back and forth" to the "mental institution" or who forced him to take "harmful drugs."

So construed, the Court will now review Plaintiff's claims (made against Defendant Butler in his individual and official capacities) to determine whether the First Amended Complaint alleges sufficient factual allegations to support a default judgment against Defendant Butler.

3. Official Capacity Claim

In his motion, Plaintiff seeks a default judgment against Defendant Butler in his official capacity.

Because Defendant Butler is a state employee under North Carolina law, Plaintiff's official capacity claim constitutes a claim against the State of North Carolina. See Graham, 473 U.S. at 165-66; see also N.C. Const. art. IV, §§ 18, 20; accord N.C. Gen. Stat. §§ 7A-60, 7A-65; see also McNair, 2012 U.S. Dist. LEXIS 99614, at *5-6. The Supreme Court has made it clear that a "state" does not qualify as a "person" for purpose of claims made pursuant to Sections 1983 or 1985. See, e.g., Will v. Mich. Dep't of State Police, 491 U.S. 58, 70-71 (1989); Mahle v. Municipality of Anchorage, 313 Fed. App'x 18, 19 (9th Cir. 2008); Ross v. Illinois, 48 Fed. App'x 200, 202 (7th Cir. 2002). Because North Carolina is not a "person" against which a Section 1983 or 1985 suit can be based. Plaintiff's official capacity claims against Defendant Butler must fail. Therefore, default judgment cannot be granted on these claims and Plaintiff's official capacity claims against Defendant Butler must be **DISMISSED**.

    4. *Individual Capacity Claim – Failure to State a Claim under 42 U.S.C. § 1985*

Plaintiff has rooted part of his First Amended Complaint on a Section 1985 claim against Defendant Butler in his individual capacity. Plaintiff's Section 1985 claim can only be premised on subsection (3) of that statute, which imposes liability upon persons who "depriv[e] ... any person ... [of] equal protection of the laws, or of equal privileges and immunities under the laws ..." See 42 U.S.C. § 1985(3). Subsections (1) and (2) are clearly inapplicable. See Bloch v. Mt Mission Sch., 1988 U.S. App. LEXIS 19712, at *2 (4th Cir. 1988) (per curiam) (discussing 42 U.S.C. § 1985(2) and describing it as prohibiting "two or more persons from conspiring to deter by force, intimidate, or threat, any party or witness from attending or testifying truthfully in a federal court" (emphasis supplied)); <u>Bald Head Ass'n</u>

<u>v. Curnin</u>, 2010 U.S. Dist. LEXIS 45737, at *15

(E.D.N.C. 2010) (discussing 42 U.S.C. § 1985(1) and

describing it as prohibiting "conspiracies to prevent a

federal officer from performing his duties or from

accepting such office"). In order to state a claim under

42 U.S.C. § 1985(3), a plaintiff must include an

allegation of "class-based, invidiously discriminatory

animus." Munson v. Friske, 754 F.2d 683, 695 (7th Cir.

1985); see also Griffin v. Breckenridge, 403 U.S. 88,

102 (1971) ("The constitutional shoals that would lie in

the path of interpreting § 1985 (3) as a general federal

tort law can be avoided by giving full effect to the

congressional purpose ... The language requiring intent

to deprive of equal protection, or equal privileges and

immunities, means that there must be some racial, or

perhaps otherwise class-based, invidiously

discriminatory animus behind the conspirators' action.").

Here, even with a liberal construction, Plaintiff's First Amended Complaint contains absolutely no factual allegations which allow this Court to plausibly infer that Defendant Butler (or any other defendant) acted with a racial or other "class-based, invidiously discriminatory animus." See generally [Doc. No. 2]. While there are allegations which somewhat refer to Plaintiff's religious proclivities and mental functioning. [Doc. No. 2]. At pp. 216, these general and nebulous allegations do not sufficiently imply – beyond a speculative level – that Defendant Butler (or others) acted with a "class-based" and "invidiously discriminatory animus" toward Plaintiff. See Iqbal, 556 U.S. at 678; Twombly, 550 U.S. at 570. Therefore, Plaintiff's First Amended Complaint fails to state an individual claim against Defendant Butler under 42 U.S.C. § 1985 and default judgment cannot be entered on such claim.

5. Individual Capacity Claim – Failure to

State a Claim under 42 U.S.C. § 1983

The Court now turns to Plaintiff's individual

Section claims against Defendant Butler. Section 1983

of Title 42 of the United States Code provides:

> Every person who, under color of any statute,
>
> ordinance, regulation, custom, or usage, of any
>
> State ..., subjects, or causes to be subjected,
>
> any citizen of the United States or other person
>
> within the jurisdiction thereof to the deprivation of
>
> any rights, privileges, or immunities secured by
>
> the Constitution and laws, shall be liable to the
>
> party injured in an action at law, suit in equity, or
>
> other proper proceeding for redress ....

42 U.S.C. § 1983, Section 1983 creates only the right of

action; it does not create any substantive rights;

instead, substantive rights must come from the

Constitution of federal statute. See Spielman v.

Hildebrand, 873 F.2d 1377, 1386 (10th Cir. 1989)

("Section 1983 does not provide a remedy if federal law

does not create enforceable rights."); see also Sawyer

v. Asbury, 537 Fed. App'x 283, 290 (4th Cir. 2013)

("Section 1983 'is not itself a source of substantive

rights,' but merely provides 'a method for vindicating

federal rights elsewhere conferred.'" (quoting Albright v.

Oliver, 510 U.S. 266, 271 (1994)). Rather, 42 U.S.C. §

1983 only authorizes an injured party to assert a claim

for relief against a person who, acting under color of

state law, violated the party's otherwise federally

secured rights.

To state a claim upon which relief can be granted

under Section 1983, a plaintiff must allege: (i) a

deprivation of a federal right; and (ii) that the person

who deprived the plaintiff of that right acted under color

of state law. See West v. Atkins, 487 U.S. 42, 48

(1988). Broken down differently, a plaintiff must establish:

> (1) A violation of rights protected by the federal Constitution or created by federal statute or regulation, (2) proximately caused (3) by the conduct of a "person" (4) who acted under color of any statute, ordinance, regulation, custom or usage, of any State or Territory or the District of Columbia.

See M. SCHWARTZ, SEC. 1983 LITTIG. CLAIMS & DEFENSES, § 1.04.

    i.   PLAINTIFF'S FIFTH AMENDMENT CLAIM.

At the outset, to the extent the First Amended Complaint attempts to allege liability against Defendant Butler under the Fifth Amendment, Plaintiff's First Amended Complaint fails to state a claim. The Fifth Amendment provides as follows:

No person shall be held to answer for a capital, or otherwise infamous crime, unless on a presentment or indictment of a Grand Jury, except in cases arising in the land or naval forces, or in the Militia, when in actual service in time of War or public danger; nor shall any person be subject for the same offence to be twice put in jeopardy of life or limb; nor shall be compelled in any criminal case to be a witness against himself, nor be deprived of life, liberty, or property, without due process of law; nor shall private property be taken for public use, without just compensation.

U.S. CONST. amend. V. The Fifth Amendment's Double Jeopardy Clause, privilege against self-incrimination, and Takings Clause are applied to the states, and their state actors, through the Fourteenth Amendment. Webb's Fabulous Pharmacies, Inc. v. Beckwith, 449 U.S. 155 (1980) (Takings Clause);

Benton v. Maryland, 395 U.S. 784 (1969) (Double Jeopardy Clause); Malloy v. Hogan. 378 U.S. 1 (1964) (privilege against self-incrimination); but see Peters v. Kiff, 407 U.S. 493 (1972) (requirement of grand jury indictment not applicable to states). "Absent incorporation through the Fourteenth Amendment, the Fifth Amendment[] ... does not proscribe conduct by state actors," and cannot, therefore supply the basis for a Section 1983 action. See Luckett v. Turner, 18 F.Supp. 2d 835, 838-39 (W.D. Tenn. 1998).

Here, all of the defendants, particularly Defendant Butler, are state actors. The Court has reviewed the First Amended Complaint earnestly and, construing Plaintiff's allegations liberally and in his favor, the Court is unable to discern any specific factual allegations that plausibly implicate a claim based on the deprivation of a Fifth Amendment right that has been incorporated against the states. Plaintiff has not alleged that he was subjected to double jeopardy, or self-incrimination. Further, his references to a deprivation of "property" are conclusory and lack factual support, and thus do not plausibly imply that a "takings" occurred.

[1] See [Doc. No. 2] at pp. 1, 5 (¶ 6), Thus, Plaintiff's First Amended Complaint fails to state a Section 1983 claim under the Fifth Amendment, and default judgment against Defendant Butler would be inappropriate on that basis.

ii.   PLAINTIFF'S FIRST, FOURTH, AND

FOURTEENTH AMENDMENT CLAIMS.

Plaintiff also alleges First, Fourth, and Fourteenth Amendment claims; however, Plaintiff does not

---

[1] This allegation is also insufficient to allege that plaintiff has been deprived of property interests without "due process of law" under either the Fifth or Fourteenth Amendments. Plaintiff has not alleged any facts indicating what property was deprived, or how it was deprived. Without further factual development, the Court cannot infer a plausible violation of the Plaintiff's substantive or procedural due process rights as they relate to this allegation. Thus, default judgment cannot be entered on this claim.

specifically tie any of his factual allegations to any
particular constitutional provision. Because of Plaintiff's
inartful pleading style, the Court believes that its
analysis will be better served by examining each of
Plaintiff's allegations to determine whether any one of
them touch upon and allege the deprivation of a
constitutional right.

Plaintiff first alleges that Defendant Butler
improperly threatened his counsel with criminal charges
if Plaintiff contested custody at his children's custody
hearing. [Doc. No.2] at pp. 2-3 (¶ 3). As a result of the
hearing, Plaintiff lost custody of his children. Id. The
Court construes this allegation as attempting to state a
claim for the denial of Plaintiff's right to meaningful
access to the courts. [1] It is well established that citizens

---

[1] The Supreme Court has not specifically determined from
which specific constitutional provision this right arises;
however, it has construed it to arise from both the First and
Fourteenth Amendments. See Christopher v. Harbury, 536 U.S.
403, 415 n. 12 (2002) (citing Bill Johnson's Restaurants, Inc. v.
NLRB, 461 U.S. 731, 741 (1983) (First Amendment); Wolff v.

have a right of access to the courts. See Christopher v. Harbury, 536 U.S. 403, 415 n.12 (2002); accord Pollard v. Pollard, 325 Fed. App'x 270, 272 (4th Cir. 2009). The right not only protects the ability to get into courts, but also ensures that such access be "adequate, effective, and meaningful." Bounds v. Smith, 430 U.S. 817, 822 (1977). The denial of meaningful access to the courts is established where a party engages in actions which effectively cover up evidence or actually render any state court remedies ineffective. Swekel v. City of River Rouge, 119 F.3d 1259, 1262 (6th Cir. 1997); accord Pollard, 325 Fed. App'x at 272. However, a "plaintiff cannot merely guess that a state court remedy will be ineffective because of a defendant's actions." Swekel, 119 F.3d at 1264. To prevail on his claims, a plaintiff

---

McDonnell, 418 U.S. 539, 576 (1974) (Fourteenth Amendment Due Process Clause); California Motor Transport Co. v. Trucking Unlimited, 404 U.S. 508, 513 (1972) (First Amendment); Boddie v. Connecticut, 401 U.S. 371, 380-381 (1971) (Fourteenth Amendment Due Process Clause)).

must demonstrate that a defendant's actions foreclosed
him from litigating in state court or rendered ineffective
any state court remedy he previously may have had. Id.
at 1263-64. A backward-looking access to courts claim,
like Plaintiff's, lies when he identifies a "specific case[]
that cannot now be tried (or tried with all material
evidence), no matter what official action may be in the
future." Christopher, 536 U.S. at 413-14. In order to
plead a backward looking denial of access to the courts
claim, a plaintiff must allege, with specificity, a "nonfrivolous" and "arguable" claim; that his remedy for that
claim has been denied and is "completely foreclosed;"
and that the defendant's actions prevented him from
litigating that claim. Id. at 415-16; Lewis v. Casey, 518
U.S. 343, 353 n.3 (1996); Broudy v. Mather, 460 F.3d
106, 120 (D.C. Cir. 2006). "[T]he predicate claim [must]
be described well enough to apply the 'nonfrivolous'
test and show that the 'arguable' nature of the

underlying claim is more than hope." <u>Christopher</u>, 536

U.S. at 416. "[I]f relief on the underlying claims is still

available in a suit that may yet be brought," then a

plaintiff's denial of access claim cannot prevail. <u>Broudy</u>,

460 F.3d at 120.

Additionally, a plaintiff "must come forward with

something more than vague and conclusory allegations

of inconvenience or delay in his instigation or

prosecution of legal actions ... The fact that a[] [plaintiff]

may not be able to litigate in exactly the manner he

desires is not sufficient to demonstrate the actual injury

element of an access to courts claim," <u>Godfrey v.</u>

<u>Wash. County</u>, 2007 U.S. Dist. LEXIS 60519, at *38-40

(W.D. Va. 2007) (citing <u>Lewis</u>, 518 U.S. at 351, 354).

Here, Plaintiff's First Amended Complaint falls far

short of stating a viable claim that he was denied

access to the courts by Defendant Butler during his

children's custody hearing. Plaintiff alleges only that

Defendant Butler threatened his *counsel* with charges

of obstruction of justice should Plaintiff participate in the

hearing – Plaintiff himself. Id. Under North Carolina law,

a custody hearing is a civil proceeding. See, e.g.,

Stancill v. Stancill, 773 S.E. 2d 890, 894, (N.C. Ct. App.

2015). A civil plaintiff is not afforded the constitutional

right to counsel. See Drostle v. Julien, 477 F.3d 1030,

1036 (8th Cir. 2007) ("In the civil context, the

constitutional right to counsel of one's own choice is not

implicated."); accord Gandy v. Reid, 505 Fed. App'x

908, 911(11th Cir. 2013); Ward v. Ortho-Mcneil Pharm,

2015 U.S. Dist. LEXIS 87848m at *5 (E,D,B,C, 2015)

("There is not constitutional right to counsel in civil

cases." (citing Cook v. Bounds, 518 F.2d 779, 780 (4th

Cir. 1975)). Thus, even assuming Defendant Butler

made the alleged threat of criminal prosecution against

Plaintiff's counsel during the custody proceedings,

Plaintiff was still free to participate in the proceedings

sans counsel. See Powell v. Gorham, 2013 U.S. Dist. LEXIS 83858, at *79 (N.D. Ala. 2013) ("[A]ny alleged threats or coercion to Plaintiffs' counsel did not inhibit their access to the courts, or constitute an obstruction of justice.").

Moreover, Plaintiff's First Amended Complaint does not allege that Defendant Butler's threat of criminal prosecution *actually prevented Plaintiff from participating in the custody hearing.* [Doc No. 2] at pp. 2-3 (¶ 3). Indeed, the First Amended Complaint appears to show, on its face, that Plaintiff *did* participate in the hearing. See id at p. 3 (¶ 3) (wherein Plaintiff describes what occurred during the proceedings). It seems clear to the Court that if the Plaintiff still participated in the custody hearing, despite the threat to his counsel, then Plaintiff was not denied access to the courts by Defendant Butler's action.

Critically, the First Amended Complaint also does not allege that Defendant Butler's actions deprived Plaintiff of any available state law remedies, such as an appeal or his right to seek a modification of custodial rights. See, e.g., N.C. Gen. Stat. §§ 7B-1000, *et seq.* Thus, the First Amended Complaint does not allege that Plaintiff's state remedies were "completely foreclosed" by Defendant Butler's actions. See Broudy, 460 F.3d at 120. Rather, at most, it alleges only that Butler's actions caused him "inconvenience or delay" in participating in his children's custody hearing. See Godfey, 2007 U.S. Dist. LEXIS 60519, at *38-40. Thus, Plaintiff's First Amended Complaint does not state a viable claim for an unconstitutional denial of access to the courts, and default judgment against Defendant Butler would be inappropriate on that basis. [1]

---

[1] To the extent Plaintiff challenges the outcome of the custody hearing, this Court is without subject matter jurisdiction to question the state court's determination. See <u>Rooker v. Fidelity Trust Co.</u>, 263 U.S. 413 (1923); District of Columbia Court of

Next, Plaintiff seems to argue that his "non-threatening freedom of speech in a religious writing" was shared with Defendant Butler without his consent and Defendant Butler used such correspondence against him in grand jury proceedings. [Doc. No. 2] at p. 3 (¶ 4). Specifically, Plaintiff claims that Defendant Butler filed "spurious and totalitarian charges" of "indecent liberties" and "statutory rape" against him by misleading a grand jury through the omission of "significant [exculpatory] information that would negate probably cause[.]" Id. at p. 4 (¶ 5). Assuming these facts to be true, Plaintiff has not stated a claim for the violation of a constitutional right. Plaintiff has not

---

Appeals v. Feldman, 460 U.S. 462 (1983); see also Adkins v. Rumsfeld, 464 F.3d 456, 463 (4th Cir. 2006) (Rooker-Feldman doctrine is jurisdictional). The Rooker-Feldman doctrine prohibits "lower federal courts ... from exercising appellate jurisdiction" respecting "state-court" judgments." See id. (quotation omitted). This prohibition extends to complaint which request a federal court to review and vacate a state court custody determination. See, generally, Stratton v. Mecklenburg County Dep't of Soc. Servs, 521 Fed Appx 278 (4th Cir. 2013).

alleged more than a conclusory statement that his writings were "religious," and he has made no allegation concerning how their "religious" nature played any part in their use before the grand jury. Further, Plaintiff has not alleged facts which plausibly imply that the "religious" nature of his writings prompted Defendant Butler to retaliate against him. Similarly, through Plaintiff conclusory alleges that his writings constituted "free speech," Plaintiff has not alleged any facts showing that Defendant Butler sought to discriminate or retaliate against him in an unconstitutional manner based only on the content of his writings, to the extent such writings were constitutionally protected. See, e.g., Hartman v. Moore, 547 U.S. 250, 256 (2006) ("Official reprisal for protected speech offends the Constitution [because] it threatens to inhibit exercise of the protected right, ... and the law is settled that as a general matter the First Amendment prohibits government officials from subjecting an individual to

retaliatory actions, including criminal prosecutions, for

speaking out ... "(internal quotation marks omitted)).

Rather, he appears to allege only that his "non-

threatening" letters should not have been presented to

the grand jury as evidence to institute criminal

proceedings without his "consent." [Doc. No. 2] at pp. 3-

4 (¶¶ 4-5).

Certain writings can form the basis of a criminal

prosecution. See, e.g., United States v. White, 670 F.3d

498, 514-15 (4th Cir. 2012) ("[S]peech is not protected

by the First Amendment when it is the very vehicle of

the crime itself." (quoting United States v. Varani, 435

F.2d 758, 762 (6th Cir. 1970)); United States v.

Meredith, 685 F.3d 814, 819 (9th Cir. 2012) ("[T]he

Supreme Court has carved out some limited categories

of 'unprotected' speech, including 'obscenity,

defamation, fraud, incitement, and speech integral to

criminal conduct.'" (quoting United States v. Stevens,

559 U.S. 460, 468-69 (2010) (citations omitted)); Rice

v. Paladin Enters, 128 F.3d 233, 245 (4th Cir. 1997)

("[W]here speech becomes an integral part of the crime,

a First Amendment defense is foreclosed even if the

prosecution rests on words along."). Thus, mere

presentment of his writings as evidence to support an

indictment is not a violation of the Constitution.

Further, it appears from the First Amended

Complaint that the writings were presented to the grand

jury as corroborating evidence to support an indictment

of "indecent liberties" and "statutory rape." Without

more facts, the Court is left to speculate about the

content of his writings. However, even if Plaintiff alleges

the writings were "non-threatening" or "religious" in

nature, the writings very well could have corroborated a

charge of "statutory rape" or other charge based on the

writings' content, when compared to other evidence

available to Defendant Butler and the grand jury. Such a use would not be an unconstitutional use of Plaintiff's writings. Thus, the First Amended Complaint fails to state a claim that Plaintiff's First Amendment rights were violated simply because Defendant Butler presented his writings to a grand jury. Default judgment, therefore, cannot be awarded on this claim.

Likewise, without more facts, Defendant Butler's receipt and use of Plaintiff's writings do not constitute an unlawful "search" under the Fourth Amendment. "An individual does not have a 'reasonable expectation of privacy' in information that is 'revealed to a third party and conveyed by him to Government authorities, even if the information is revealed on the assumption that it will be used only for a limited purpose and the confidence placed in the third party will not be betrayed.'" United States v. Shah, 2015 U.S. Dist. LEXIS 826, at *14-15 (E.D.N.C 2015) (quoting United States v. Miller, 425

U.S. 435, 443 (1976)); accord Manning v. Ross, 2013

U.S. Dist. LEXIS 125992, at *24-25 (M.D. Pa. 2013)

("First and foremost, from what can be gleaned from the

facts provided by Plaintiff, the letters that led to the

arrest [of] Plaintiff were handed to Defendants by

Pamela Ross, and, therefore, because they were in the

possession of a third party, i.e. Pamela Ross, Plaintiff

did not retain a reasonable expectation of privacy in

these letters.").

Here, Plaintiff alleges that he sent his letters to the

children's guardian ad litem, and the guardian ad litem

then turned them over to Defendant Butler. Because

Plaintiff gave the letters the guardian ad litem – i.e., a

third party – Plaintiff retained no reasonable expectation

of privacy in them. Thus, the letters could lawfully be

turned over to Defendant Butler by the guardian ad

litem for Defendant to use as he wished. For this

reason, the First Amended Complaint fails to state a

claim that Plaintiff's Fourth Amendment rights were violated simply because a third party, to whom Plaintiff sent letters, disclosed those letters to a prosecutor without Plaintiff's consent. The Court cannot enter default judgment on this claim.

Additionally, Plaintiff makes an amorphous claim that his constitutional rights were violated because Defendant Butler "misled" a grand jury by not disclosing what Plaintiff contends to be exculpatory information during the grand jury's proceedings. However, the Constitution does not require a prosecutor to disclose exculpatory information during grand jury proceedings. See e.g., United States v. Williams, 504 U.S. 36, 51-52 (1992) ("it is axiomatic that the grand jury sits not to determine guilt or innocence, but to assess whether there is adequate basis for bringing a criminal charge. That has always been no; and to make the assessment it has always been though sufficient to hear only the prosecutor's side ... [In the United States,] the suspect

under investigation by the grand jury [has] [n]ever been

thought to have a right to testify or to have exculpatory

evidence presented."); United States v. Witasick, 443

Fed. App'x 838, 843 (4th Cir 2011) (recognizing that the

Supreme Court has unequivocally held that "'[i]mposing

upon the prosecutor a legal obligation to present

exculpatory evidence in his possession would be

incompatible with [the adversarial] system.'" (quoting

Williams, 504 U.S. at 52)). Here, Plaintiff's claim falls

squarely within Williams and Witasick and must be

rejected. Because the First Amended Complaint does

not state a claim that Defendant Butler's failure to

provide exculpatory information to the grand jury

violated Plaintiff's constitutional rights, default judgment

on this claim is improper.

To the extent Plaintiff attempts to allege that the

"indecent liberties" and "statutory rape" charges were

not based on probably cause, and thus violated the Fourth Amendment, this claim also fails. It is clear from the First Amended Complaint that these charges were brought pursuant to a grand jury indictment. A grand jury indictment establishes the existence of probable cause as a matter of law. See, e.g., Giordenello v. United States, 357 U.S. 480, 487 (1958); Campbell v. City of San Antonio, 43 F.3d 973, 976 (5th Cir. 1995) (nothing that an arrest warrant may be based on a grand jury indictment which establishes probable cause); accord Durham v. Horner, 690 F.3d 183, 188-89 (4th Cir. 2012) ("Durham is unable to establish a constitutional violation because, although the underlying criminal proceedings were terminated in his favor, the prosecution was plainly supported by probable cause, as conclusively established by the three indictments. It has long since been settled by the Supreme Court that 'an indictment, fair upon its face, returned by a properly constituted grand jury, conclusively determines the existence of probable cause." (quoting Gerstein v. Pugh, 420 U.S. 103, 117 n.19 (1975)). Here, Plaintiff has not alleged any facts that lead to the plausible conclusion that the grand jury's indictment, charging him with "indecent liberties" and "statutory rape," were not properly based upon probable cause. Thus, the First Amended Complaint fails to state a claim and default judgment against Defendant Butler should not be entered on this issue.

Plaintiff's First Amended Complaint also makes a general allegation that, in October 2007, Defendant Butler unlawfully charged him with "fraudulently burning [a] dwelling." [Doc. No. 2] at p. 5 (¶ 6). He claims that this charge was unlawful because "higher State Courts previously held that charge does not apply when no substantial harm" occurs to another's property or where insurance fraud does not result.

However, the First Amended Complaint fails to cite any authority for these legal assertions and it utterly fails to allege any facts that plausibly imply that the charge was not based upon probable cause. This Court will not speculate as to whether Plaintiff's conclusory allegations of unlawful conduct rise to the level of plausibility. See Iqbal, 556 U.S. at 678; Twombly, 550 U.S. at 570. Therefore, the Court does not find that this allegation states a claim and will not enter default judgment against Defendant Butler on that basis.

Moreover, the First Amended Complaint alleges that, while Plaintiff was in state custody between 2009 and 2012, he was unlawfully transferred "back and forth" to a "mental institution" and forced to take "harmful drugs." [Doc. No. 2] at pp. 5-6 (¶¶ 7-8). Notably, Plaintiff does *not* argue that his actual confinement during that period was unconstitutional. Even assuming his allegations are sufficient to claim the deprivation of a constitutional right, Plaintiff has not alleged any facts which plausibly imply that Defendant Butler *caused* Plaintiff to be transferred to the "mental institution" or forced him to take "harmful drugs." The absence of any well-pleaded facts supporting this casual relation is fatal to Plaintiff's claim against Defendant Butler. As a result, the Court declines to enter default judgment against Defendant Butler on this basis.

iii. PLAINTIFF'S "INTERNATIONAL HUMAN RIGHTS CLAIM.

Finally, Plaintiff has alleged that Defendant Butler violated his rights under "International Human Rights." [Doc. No. 2] at p. 1. However, Plaintiff's First Amended Complaint fails to cite this Court to any treaty or executive agreement of the United States that affords Plaintiff rights that may be vindicated in a Section 1983 action. Additionally, he has alleged no facts supporting the violation of any such treaty or executive agreement. Therefore, the First Amended Complaint fails to state a claim and default judgment may not be entered on this claim.

iv.   CONCLUSION

The Court has extensively and painstakingly reviewed each and every individualized claim against Defendant Butler that can be reasonably deduced from Plaintiff's First Amended Complaint. Finding that none of the claims asserted state a claim against Defendant Butler, the Court concludes that it would be improper to grant Plaintiff's motion for default judgement against him in his individual capacity. Accordingly, the Court **DENIES** Plaintiff's Motion for Default Judgment against Defendant Butler.

6. Leave to File Second Amended Complaint. When a district court is inclined to dismiss a complaint for failure to state a claim, the court "should consider

granting the plaintiff, and in particular, a pro se plaintiff, leave to amend his complaint." Fisher v. Winston-Salem Police Dep't, 28 F.Supp. 3d 526, 533 (M.D.N.C 2014) (citing Ostrzenski v. Seigel, 177 F.3d 245, 252-53 (4th Cir. 1999)). Unless it is certain that a plaintiff cannot state a claim upon amendment to the complaint, then "the better practice is to allow at least one amendment" Id. (quoting Ostrzenski, 177 F.3d at 253). The Fourth Circuit has held that "*pro se* litigants are entitled to explicit notice of the consequences of various legal actions." See Carter v. Hutto, 781 F.2d 1028, 1033 (4th Cir. 1986); Wright v. Collins, 766 F.2d 841, (4th Cir. 1985); Roseboro v. Garrison, 528 F.2d 309 (4th Cir. 1975). However, this Court is neither required nor permitted to "bend the substantive requirements" faced by all litigants when "wading into the world of federal litigation" – *pro se* or not. See Williams v. Wicomico

County Bd. Of Educ., 2012 U.S. Dist. LEXIS 141665, at
*8 (D.Md. 2012).

Because the Court has engaged in a *sua sponte*
analysis of Plaintiff's First Amended Complaint in order
to determine whether Plaintiff has stated a claim
against Defendant Butler upon which a default
judgment may be entered, the Court, in its discretion,
has determined equity requires that it give the Plaintiff
notice of its decision and an opportunity to file a second
amended complaint. See, e.g., Singleton v. Dean, 611
Fed. App'x 671, 671 (11th Cir. Aug. 4, 2015) ("Prior to
dismissing an action *sua sponte* [based on the district
court's determination that, after a review of the
complaint's allegation, default judgment is not
warranted], a court must provide the plaintiff with notice
of its intent to dismiss and an opportunity to respond."
(citing Surtain, 789 F.3d at 1248)). Plaintiff may utilize
this opportunity by attempting to correct any of the

deficiencies highlighted in this Court's Order. However, the Court has determined only that Plaintiff should be given an opportunity to cure the deficiencies in his First Amended Complaint. Further, the Court will not permit Plaintiff an opportunity to amend his "official capacity" claims against Defendant Butler because those claims are claims against the state itself and the deficiencies surrounding them are incapable of being rendered.

Accordingly, as it relates to Defendant Butler, the Court declines to dismiss the First Amended Complaint outright and *in toto*. Instead, the Plaintiff is **GRANTED LEAVE** to file a second amended complaint within **THIRTY (30) DAYS** of the date of this Court's Order. If Plaintiff chooses to file a second amended complaint within the prescribed timeframe, then the second amended complaint *must* be served upon all parties against whom the Plaintiff alleges a claim. This includes, but is not limited to, the City of Statesville,

See Fed. R. Civ. Pro. 4(j)(2). Failure to serve all parties

may result in the summary dismissal of Plaintiff's claims

against any such entity. See Fed. R. Civ. Pro. 4(m); see

also Section II.C., *infra*. If Plaintiff chooses to file a

second amended complaint, Plaintiff is also **DIRECTED**

to closely follow and abide by the requirements of Rule

8 and 10 of the Federal Rules of Civil Procedure, which

require Plaintiff's specific claims to be alleged

separately and distinctly in numbered paragraphs and

counts, and which require Plaintiff to specifically identify

each defendant against whom his claims are made.

See Fed. R. Civ. Pro. 8(a) & (d); Fed. R. Civ. Pro. 10.

If Plaintiff chooses not to file a second amended

complaint within the prescribed timeframe, then this

Order will operate to dismiss all claims contained in the

First Amended Complaint that are alleged against

Defendant Butler in his individual capacity. Further, this

Order will operate to dismiss Plaintiff's claims against

the City, as provided below. See Fed. R. Civ. Pro.

4(j)(2) & (m); Section II.C., *infra*. Finally, the

Department and Defendant Wall will be allowed to

renew their motion to dismiss the First Amended

Complaint at that time. See Section II.B., *infra*.

B. Defendants' Motion to Dismiss

This Order has not analyzed any of Plaintiff's

claims as they relate to the Department or Defendant

Wall because such defendants were not the object of

Plaintiff's motion for default judgment. The Court

acknowledges that the Department and Defendant Wall

have filed a motion to dismiss on statute of limitations

grounds. [Doc. No. 5]. The Court further acknowledges

that some of the claims alleged against Defendant

Butler may be implicated in Plaintiff's claims against the

Department or Defendant Wall; however, neither the

Department nor Defendant Wall moved to dismiss on

the grounds discussed herein. Nevertheless, the Court

finds that, because of its holding in Section II.A., *supra*, it is inappropriate to rule on Defendants' motion to dismiss at this time. This is because Plaintiff could amend his complaint to such a degree that the Defendants' motion to dismiss is either mooted or refuted. Accordingly, the Court **DENIES WITHOUT PREJUDICE** Defendants' motion to dismiss. [Doc. No. 5]. Should Plaintiff file a second amended complaint within the prescribed time, the Defendants may then file a motion to dismiss that complaint. Should Plaintiff fail to file a second amended complaint, then the Defendants are granted leave to re-file their motion to dismiss upon the Plaintiff's failure to do so.

C. Plaintiff's Claim Against the City

Plaintiff has also named the City of Statesville as a defendant in this lawsuit; however, the docket shows that service has never been perfected on the City. The Court declines to review the viability of any claims asserted in the First Amended Complaint against the City because the record clearly shows that the City has not been served. Plaintiff's proposed order, filed with his motion for default judgment, appears to also request a default judgment against the City. However, the City has not been served and the Court cannot, therefore, grant any affirmative relief against it. Thus, if the Plaintiff chooses to file a second amended complaint and continue asserting a claim against the City, the Plaintiff must serve the City in accordance with the Rules. See Fed. R. Civ. Pro. 4(j)(2). If Plaintiff fails to serve the City with the second amended complaint, or fails to file a second amended complaint, then his claims against the City will be dismissed. See Fed. R. Civ. Pro. 4(m).

III. DECRETAL

IT IS, THEREFORE, ORDERED THAT:

(1) Plaintiff's Motion for Default Judgment is **DENIED**;

(2) Defendant's Motion to Dismiss is **DENIED WITHOUT PREJUDICE**;

(3) Plaintiff's "official capacity" claims against Defendant Butler are **DISMISSED WITH PREJUDICE**;

(4) Plaintiff's is **GRANTED LEAVE** to file a second amended complaint within **THIRTY (30) DAYS** of this order;

(5) The Clerk is **ORDERED** to mail, via certified mail return receipt requested, a copy of this Order to each of the named individual defendants, as well as the City of Statesville, and the Iredell County District Attorney's Office. The Clerk shall mail the Order to the attention of the officer(s) or employee(s) holding the position identified in Rule 4(j)(2)

of the Federal Rules of Civil Procedure and

N.C. Gen. Stat. § 1A-1, Rule 4(j)(5),

specifically as follows: (1) to the City of

Statesville – Mayor Costi Kutteh, P.O.Box

1111, Statesville, N.C. 28687-1111; and (2)

to the Iredell County District Attorney's Office

– District Attorney Sarah Kirkman, Iredell

County Hall of Justice Annex, 201 East Water

Street, Statesville, N.C. 28677.

SO ORDERED.

Signed: February 3, 2016

Richard L. Voorhees

United States District Judge.

APPENDIX II

IN THE UNITED STATES DISTRICT COURT

FOR THE WESTERN DISTRICT OF NORTH CAROLINA

STATESVILLE DIVISION

CIVIL ACTION NO. 5:15-CV-00083-RLV-DCK

DAVID THOMAS SILVERS, SR.,   )

    Plaintiff,   )

    v.   ) **ORDER**

IREDELL COUNTY DEPARTMENT)

OF SOCIAL SERVICES ; D.S.S. DIR)

DONALD C. WALL, IN HIS   )

INDIVIDUAL AND OFFICIAL   )

CAPACITIES; ASST. D.A. PAXTON)

BUTLER, IN HIS INDIVIDUAL AND)

OFFICIAL CAPACITIES, AND THE)

CITY OF STATESVILLE, N.C.,   )

    Defendants.   )

_____)

THIS MATTER IS BEFORE THE COURT on

Defendant Donald C. Wall's Renewed Motion to

Dismiss (the "Motion") [1] [Doc. No. 29]. Plaintiff has filed

a memorandum in opposition to the Motion. [Doc. No.

31]. The Motion was filed pursuant to the Court's

previous order on Plaintiff's Motion for Default

Judgment. [Doc. No. 20]; *see Silvers v. Iredell Cty.*

Dep't of Soc. Servs., No. 5:15-CV-00083-RLV-DCK,

2016 WL 427953 (W.D.N.C. Feb. 3, 2016) (Voorhees,

J.). This matter is now ripe for disposition.

I. BACKGROUND

The relevant factual and procedure posture of this

case is more fully set out in the Court's February 3,

2016 order. *See* [Doc. No. 20] at pp.1-5; *Silvers*, 2016

WL 427953, at *1-3. In that order, the Court determined

that Plaintiff's First Amended Complaint failed to state a

---

[1] The Motion is brought by Defendant Wall in his official and individual capacities. *See* [Doc. No. 30] at p. 1 n. 1.

claim against Defendant Paxton Butler in both his individual and official capacities. Further, the Court determined that Plaintiff had failed to serve the City of Statesville. The Court granted Plaintiff leave to file a second amended complaint in an attempt to cure his deficiencies. The Court denied Defendant Wall's first motion to dismiss, *without prejudice*, because leave was granted to Plaintiff to amend his complaint. The Plaintiff chose not to file a second amended complaint. *See* [Doc. No. 21]. Since that time, Defendant Wall has renewed his motion to dismiss on statutory limitations grounds. [Doc. No. 29].

II. DISCUSSION

A.   Standard of Review

When reviewing a Rule 12(b)(6) motion to dismiss, this Court must examine the legal sufficiency of the complaint; it may not resolve factual disputes or weigh the claims and defenses against one another. *See*

Edwards v. City of Goldsboro, 178 F.3d 231, 243 (4th

Cir. 1999). Rather, the court must accept as true all of

the well-plead factual allegations contained in the

complaint. *See Mylan Labs., Inc. v. Matkari*, 7 F.3d

1130, 1134 (4th Cir. 1993). A court may, however,

determine whether the facts alleged are sufficient, when

taken at face-value, to reasonably imply liability on the

part of the defendant. In order to survive such a motion,

the complaint's "[f]actual allegations must be enough to

raise a right to relieve above the speculative level." *Bell*

Atlantic Corp. v. Twombly, 550 U.S. 544, 555 (2007).

Indeed, the "complaint must contain sufficient factual

matter, accepted as true, to 'state a claim to relief that

is plausible on its face." *Ashcroft v. Iqbal*, 556 U.S. 662,

678 (2009) (quoting *Twombly*, 550 U.S. at 570). A claim

is facially plausible when the factual content allows for

the reasonable inference that the defendant is liable for

the misconduct alleged. *Id.*

However, a pleading that offers mere "labels and conclusions" or "a formulaic recitation of the elements of a cause of action will not do." *Iqbal*, 556 U.S. at 678. In order to assert a claim for relief, the complaint must allege facts that imply more than a "sheer possibility that a defendant has acted unlawfully" or "facts that imply more than a "sheer possibility that a defendant has acted unlawfully" or "facts that are 'merely consistent with' a defendant's liability[.]" *Id.* At 678 (quoting Twombly, 550 U.S. at 557). Critically, "'[t]he presence ... of a few conclusory legal terms does not insulate a complaint from dismissal ... when the facts alleged in the complaint' cannot support the legal conclusion" alleged or the relief sought. *See Migdal v. Rowe Price-Fleming Int'l*, 248 F.3d 321, 326(4th Cir. 2001) (quoting *Young v. City of Mount Ranier*, 238 F.3d 567, 577 (4th Cir. 2001)). "Legal inferences drawn from the facts, unwarranted inferences, unreasonable conclusions, or arguments are not part of the [court's] consideration." *Dolgaleva v. Va. Beach City Pub. Sch.,* 364 Fed. App'x 820, 827 (4th Cir. 2010); *see also Eastern Shore Mkts., Inc. v. J.D. Assocs. LLP,* 213 F.3d 175, 180 (4th Cir. 2000).

In applying this standard, the Supreme Court has reiterated that "[a] document filed *pro se* is to be liberally construed and a *pro se* complaint, however inartfully pleaded, must be held to less stringent standards than formal pleadings drafted by lawyers." *Erickson v. Pardus,* 551 U.S. 89, 94 (2007) (internal citations and quotation marks omitted); *Dolgaleva,* 364 Fed. App'x at 827. However, the Fourth Circuit has "not read *Erickson* to undermine *Twombly's* requirement that a pleading contain more than labels and conclusions[.]" *Giarratano v. Johnson,* 521 F.3d 298, 304 n.5 (4th Cir. 2008) (internal quotation marks omitted) (applying *Twombly* standard in dismissing *pro se* complaint; *accord Atherton v. Dist. Of Columbia Off. Of Mayor,* 567 F.3d 672, 681-82(D.C. Cir. 2009) ("A *pro se* complaint ... 'must be held to less stringent standards than formal pleadings drafted by lawyers.' But even a *pro se* complainant must plead 'factual matter' that permits the court to infer 'more than the mere possibility of misconduct.'" (quoting *Erickson,* 551 U.S. at 94; *Iqbal,* 556 U.S. at 679)). The rules governing the generous construction of *pro se* pleadings "do[] not relieve the plaintiff of the burden of alleging sufficient facts on which a recognized legal claim could be based." *Ashby v. City of Charlotte,* 2015 U.S. Dist. LEXIS 103286, at *4 (W.D.N.C. Aug, 6, 2015); *Godfrey v. Long,* 2012 U.S. Dist. LEXIS 2671, at *3-4 (E.D.N.C. 2012) quoting *Hall v. Bellmon,* 935 F.2d 1106, 1110 (10th Cir. 1901)).

B. <u>Plaintiff's Claims Against Defendant Butler and the City of Statesville</u>

In its prior order, the Court warned Plaintiff that, should he fail to file a second amended complaint, his First Amended Complaint would be subject to dismissal as to Defendant Butler and the City of Statesville for the reasons discussed herein. The prior order dismissed, *with prejudice* Plaintiff's claims against Defendant Butler in his official capacity. *See* [Doc. No. 20] at p. 34; *Silvers,* 2016 WL 427953, at *17. In accordance with the Court's prior order, and for the reasons stated therein, the Court now **DISMISSES WITH PREJUDICE** Plaintiff's claims against Defendant Butler, in his individual capacity, and the City of Statesville. *See* [Doc. No. 20]; *Silvers v. Iredell Cty. Dep't of Soc. Servs.,* No. 5:15-CV-000083-RLV-DCK, 2016 WL 427953 (W.D.N.C. Feb 3, 2016).

C. Plaintiff's Claims Against Defendant Wall

Defendant Wall, in his individual and official capacity, moves to dismiss Plaintiff's claims against him and the Iredell County Department of Social Services (hereinafter, the "Department") on statute of limitations grounds. Plaintiff has alleged a conglomeration of federal civil rights claims against Defendant Wall and the Department under Sections 1983 and 1985 of Title 42 of the United States Code. *See* 42 U.S.C. §§ 1983, 1985; *see also* [Doc. No. 2] at p. 1. Defendant Wall argues that the First Amended Complaint alleges wrongful acts by him and the Department dating no later than 2004. *See* [Doc. No. 30] at p. 5. Therefore, Defendant argues, it is "clearly apparent" from the face of the complaint that Plaintiff's claims against him and the Department are time-barred because this action was not instituted until June 2015. *See id.* Neither Section 1983 nor Section 198 contain a statute of limitations – therefore, "courts borrow the statute of limitations from the most analogous state-law cause of action." *Owens v. Baltimore City State's Attorneys*

Office, 767 F.3d 379, 388 (4th Cir. 2014), *cert. denied sub nom. Baltimore City Police Dep't v. Owens*, 135 S. Ct. 1893, 191 L. Ed. 2d 762 (2015). In civil rights cases, the Supreme Court and the circuit courts have counseled that district courts should apply the statute of limitations applicable to state-law personal injury actions. *See Owens v. Okure*, 488 U.S. 235, 249-50, 109 S.Ct. 573, 102 L.Ed.2d 594 (1989); *Owens v. Baltimore City State's Attorneys Office*, 767 F.3d 379, 388 (4th Cir. 2014); *see also Lake v. Arnold*, 232 F.3d 360, 368 (3d Cir. 2000) (for both § 1983 and § 1985 claims, the court "look[s] to the general, residual statute of limitations for personal injury actions"); *Rozar v. Mullis*, 85 F.3d 556, 561 (11th Cir. 1996) (same); *McDougal v. County of Imperial*, 942 F.2d 668, 673 (9th Cir. 1991) (same). Under North Carolina law, the appropriate statute of limitations is the three-year period prescribed by N.C. Gen. Stat. § 1-52.

"A motion to dismiss based on a ... statute of limitations should not be granted unless the pleadings construed in the light most favorable to a plaintiff show as a matter of law that the applicable period for filing suit has expired." *Ball v. Quorum Health Res., Inc.*, 23 F.3d 399, 1994 WL 15945, at *2 (4th Cir. 1994). Here, the Court has reviewed the First Amended Complaint closely and concludes that Defendant is correct; Plaintiff last alleges that Defendant Wall caused a direct violation of his civil rights on June 5, 2004. See [Doc. No. 2] at pp. 2-3 (¶ 3). There, Plaintiff alleges that Defendant Wall and the Department illegally "suppressed" his freedom of speech while visiting with his children, who were in state custody at the time. *Id.* Plaintiff filed this action long after the events of that day. *See* [Doc. No. 1].

In his opposition papers, Plaintiff claims that the statute of limitations was tolled because of his subsequent incarceration. However, the Court has reviewed the complaint alleging further dates of incarceration, and has similarly failed to submit any other materials that might be indicative of a disability sufficient to toll the statute of limitations. Therefore, it appears that "the applicable period for filing suit has expired," as a matter of law, with respect to Defendant Wall and the Department's conduct as of June 5, 2004 and before. *Ball*, 23 F.3d 399, 1994 WL 159451, at *2. Accordingly, Plaintiff's claims against Defendant Wall and the Department are **DISMISSED WITH PREJUDICE**.

To the extent Plaintiff also argues that Defendant Wall and the Department violated the Plaintiff's rights by way of a conspiracy with Defendant Butler, those claims against Defendant Butler do not state a claim upon which relief may be granted. See [Doc. No. 20]; *Silvers v. Iredell Cty. Dep't of Soc. Servs.*, No. 5:15-CV-

00083-RLV-DCK, 2016 WL 427953 (W.D.N.C. Feb. 3, 2016).

CONCLUSION

As is discussed in this order and the Court's prior order, dated February 3, 2016, the Court finds that each and every one of Plaintiff's claims against the defendants must be dismissed, *with prejudice.* Accordingly, Plaintiff's First Amended Complaint must be dismissed.

III. DECRETAL

IT IS, THEREFORE, ORDERED THAT

(1) Defendant Wall's Motion to Dismiss (Doc. No. 29) is hereby **GRANTED**;

(2) Plaintiff's First Amended Complaint (Doc. No. 2) is hereby **DISMISSED WITH PREJUDICE** in accordance with this order and the Court's February 3, 2016 order (Doc. No. 20);

(3) The Clerk shall enter judgment in favor of the

defendants, against the Plaintiff, and shall

administratively terminate this case.

SO ORDERED.

Signed: April 15, 2016

Richard L. Voorhees

United States District Judge

APPENDIX III

The following document was copyrighted by David Thomas Silvers Sr. on September 25th 2016 and then sent prior to October to the local newspaper: Statesville Record and Landmark in Statesville, North Carolina.

Oral Argument Considerations

In order to understand the offensive habitual aftermath, the offensive pre-math needs consideration. The mother of my children whom caused the offensive aftermath with the Iredell County Department of Social Services and representatives of the City of Statesville, N.C. neglected the highest Courts of law from the State of Maryland that already decided that their mother was negligent when in the first custody hearing the Circuit Court of Baltimore County Maryland ruled in their father's favor while the foregoing included their father's testimony under oath surpassing cross examination, therefore, any belated discussion about my life or my family prior to that testimony should not be considered. Their mother's wretched disorder before and after my custody to regain custody was for my sons to barbarically misbehave and wait until their father spanked them and then she would complain to Social Services. On the first day of judicial custody, my sons barbarically misbehaved upon their mother's request while their father let them exhaust themselves on the several hour drive to another State, just like in the aftermath when I let the representatives of Statesville, N.C. exhaust themselves then I moved to another State. On the first day of their father's custody, and after my wife discovered their barbarism, she started writing a daily journal. A month later, their wretched mother pleaded with my sons to tell lies about their father to the school guidance counselor while their mother called Social Services, and then the guidance counselor called their father into school and after their father told the guidance counselor what their mother was doing the social worker in Winston-Salem, N.C. closed the case. A few months later after father had built a good bond with his sons and their mother could no longer brainwash my sons, their mother turned her attention to my youngest daughter and tried to brainwash her, then after my youngest daughter visited her mother she came home depressed and stayed depressed for several days, and then after their father told his wife to take his daughter to a psychologist and she did, and then when that did not help, that is when this father and my youngest daughter became close, and that is when my youngest daughter became the most improved of my children. The intruders neglect and do not want what happens when a father cares for his daughter which helps his daughter find someone whom cares for her. When a father cares for his daughter, his fellow men think he is less of a man,

when privacy separations is what prevents the conflicts

of interest from opposing intentions from father or men,

and while her father's intentions were always regarding

care for his daughter, the intentions of men was about

sex and their inquisition of thereof proves thereof, and

when a father cares for his daughter his fellow men

think he is not caring for his sons, when their father

spent more time with his sons than his daughters.

There was extraordinary care and achievements for

everyone in my family well before others intruded while

the intruders were only interested in their degenerative

perversions.

If there was a man with a woman, and after she

expressed that she wanted him in poetic form, and then

she was satisfied and sincerely promised before visiting

others, and then smeared him after visiting others, then

that man would state she is a wrong, and if I went with

"all men are created equal", - Declaration of

Independence 1776, then every man would self-

evidently state she is wrong, although, since she is my

daughter with what was at the time minimal experience,

and since I knew she would not have slandered her

father if it was not for her wretched mother using sleazy

vulgar gossiping trash, then my daughter can be

forgiven while their mother, Iredell County Department

of Social Services, and the City of Statesville are

wrong, and while the justice system should consider

Shakespeare as it relates to age and poetic form,

thereof was surpassed with achievements that are

greater than Shakespeare since obtrusive and vicarious

plays are less worthy when surpassed from

achievements while their father taught his sons better

from a sired gender balance and merited functional

family through care, achievements, obligation, and tie

while all she had to accomplish was care for him and

his children, and then return his children to their biological father while the aftermath was about who's children are they when the children are not the property of the City, County, State, or Country, they are more the biological father and biological mother's children than anyone else's children while thereof is supported with the Ten Commandments, and then when their fatherless mother did not know how to care while his children were having nightmares, flunking, plunder from school and younger than teenagers in a gang stage while running the streets at all hours of the night, and then after their father corrects the foregoing, their fatherless mother has his children scandalously slander their father after adulteresses gossip with one another because they are crooked and more interested in pandering and salacious profiteering when in a gang stage of dysfunctional sleazy trash while degenerating civilization and population.

I did not need nor wanted belated intrusions from others unmerited dysfunctional families compelling my family to poetically or dramatically entertain others when while my daughter presented poetry to her father, her father maintained domestic tranquility with consistent achievements and her virginity as a natural form of contraception with a right "relating to marriage procreation, contraception, family relationships, and child rearing and education", - U.S. Supreme Court, Paul v. Davis 1976, while the foregoing was mostly from experiencing that most modern teenage relationships fail while an inexperienced teenage girl can become suicidal if her boyfriend breaks up with her when her father made sure that did not happen by caring for her rather than the modern world where many only want him or her for sex and their inquisition of thereof with their pandering, pornography, and salacious profiteering prove thereof while their inquisition is void of family, care, and achievements while their salacious desires lead to abortion.

When a father sires sons he must demonstrate living proof of love for his sons, and when their mother is neglectful and not present in the house, their father adapted his daughter while expressing love with prudent separation for his sons while supporting his loving daughter until death do they part. The foregoing is similar from a father and mother whom separate their personal lives from their children while the intruders have degenerated the natural separations that should happen in every household. If the foregoing is not respected and there are no family considerations nor religion nor achievements nor rules of civil procedure, then everyone will have to make an immediate choice of bearing arms or proving physicality by barbarically fighting their way through the inner-city streets and a gladiator forum of mob-rule from the negligence of representatives, Social Services, and the City. The general population continues disregarding a census gender count when a sired gender balance and merited functional family can extrapolate out to greatness while others belatedly and contentiously debate U.S. Constitutional Amendments regardless of the foregoing and regardless of the injustices stated in entry 35 of the Federal District Court.

I do not appreciate others whom use only "he said, she said" as precedence to intrude when the intruders in the middle of "he said, she said" brainwashed and coerced what "she said". Others cannot brainwash and coerce everyone with their impotent opposition and extraneous rhetoric after only conjecturing and profiteering while depriving substantive due process. If my daughter would have returned after her visit with her mother then I am sure we would have agreed on a gradual detachment from a related graduation. After others objected with their impotent, inexperienced, and zealous attempt for a truth that the intruders could not compute, they caused immediate separation anxiety and abrupt detachment disorder in my children while afflicting borderline personality disorder in my daughter and then my sons became juvenile delinquents when relying on popularly elected intruders of mob-rule and followers thereof rather than a sired gender balance and merited functional family. Their father would rather secure his sired gender balance and merited functional family rather than play belated political games with intruders. After others attempted to rewind with a harsh inquisition and linguistic barbarism, they attempted to deflect their abuse using irony when others offensive oratory was from using an insensible age of sixteen without considering precociousness and Shakespeare that considered fertility at age thirteen while their father disagreed with thirteen knowing that unemployed teenage pregnancies are not as successful since most teenagers cannot adequately support one another and have to rely on a socialistic welfare-state that causes substantial tax burdens on others.

While their mother called during the father and daughter relationship persuading father to spend more time with daughter, I made the final decision with the intent of maintaining domestic tranquility in the home for continued success, however, those that work for Social Services are not concerned about success and advancement of civilization because they are unskilled workers that receive a paycheck from a socialistic welfare-state that plunder intellectual properties then attempt to make slaves out of fathers.

I preferred privacy and tranquility without having to represent the worst example of Democracy as a politician that states insults and indignities against another politician rather than exchange policy improvements from a sired gender balance and merited functional family that will dismisses others unmerited dysfunctional imbalance and sleazy gossiping trash from an unskilled socialistic welfare-state.

I should not be compelled to publish lyrics from others to demonstrate normalcy that prefers parsing emotions to determine what is normal rather than parsing superior achievements, nor compelled to leave personal and private lyrics in my family open to the inexperienced interpretations of those not directly involved, nor compelled to submit to others impotency after siring a gender balance and merited functional family.

When arguing in public court appointed and elected from popular public opinion the choice is either demonstrate equilibrium and hope that there is a competent judge, or move the family before Democracy invades and wastes time challenging and antagonizing equilibrium when a move should have happened after equilibrium and before Democracy invaded after they listened to a wretched mother and salacious profiteers with unskilled and unskillful smear campaigns.

On July 12th, 2016, two U.S. Marshalls from North Carolina paid me a visit, and were concerned about the last sentence in my April 4th 2016 writing to the Federal District Judge that is as follows: "and if not respected, I advise the U.S. Second Amendment and go out with guns a blazing." After I thoroughly expressed my position, and the consequences of voiding the U.S. First Amendment leaving only the U.S. Second Amendment, of which I expressed should be from a well-regulated militia, and while they were not aware of any Court filings after April 4th, 2016, and my intention of filing in the U.S. Supreme Court if the Appeal to the Fourth Circuit Court is denied, the U.S.

Marshalls were pleased that I was resolving this matter civilly rather than violently.

In 1776 American men came together and unanimously dissolved political bands for the respect of mankind, then after needing a government, men chose a Democracy of men, although, since not every opinion was unanimous, men secured rights against tyranny of the majority, of which tyranny of the majority becomes more prevalent when those that were not present excessively entangle while an Athenian Democracy extraneously interferes. After the City of Statesville North Carolina intruded then they can be considered as an Athenian Democracy of WII Germany with reckless disregard for private property rights, separation, and well-being.

A father usually makes private rules in his house while most of those rules are from his interpretation from the religion of his choice through the free exercise of religion, and when his children learn from their father's rules, then it is highly likely that they will abide by the rules of public law since some public laws are more liberal. For example, permitting unemployed 13 year olds to propagate, or giving 16 year olds emancipation when they are void of an education.

The community in Statesville N.C. respected my family before representatives of the City of Statesville invaded privacy and attempted to vicariously parse a vernacular and judge emotions without firsthand sentiments and then treacherously debauched my daughter while making my sons traitors. If others did not excessively entangle and extraneously interfere, my daughter would have returned a virgin rather than others politically running off at the mouth in public while smearing and vacillating to get votes then compromising their family, their morals, and their values. Life is not that difficult if a man asks her father for her hand in marriage since her father can understand mankind since he was in the same position before he became a father, although beware, since her father will reject him if he does not significantly care while the foregoing is not based on political monetary policy since if he can care and barter, whether with monetary policy, or off the grid, care and barter is more important than others money.

After others did not reject to another debauching my daughter and taking my sons while unreasonably and incomprehensibly stating that her father is not right, their opposition was nothing more than others deflecting their degenerative perversions and invasions of privacy to take my sons and my daughter's virginity without marrying her while thinking that was right when her father's relationship with his daughter started when she was in her mother's womb while their relationship with my daughter started by attacking her father, and then after the attack, there were some that wanted to assist me and I worked with them because I believed that their intent was to reunite my family, however, I discovered many were spurious imposters attempting to stereotype and then stigmatize another when a stereotype does not apply when there were exceptional and extraordinary conditions with respectable achievements for everyone in my trust.

The problem with criminals is that they are mostly from fatherless homes while some public laws are what can ironically cause violence, and when fatherless homes are mostly in the City, more laws are broken in the City with unacceptable murders that prove thereof. The reality is my children achieved more harmless success under my private rules than under belated rules of public law that harmed while the wasted time from others invasions of privacy is the most of all disappointments.

I had never thought about killing another until after invasions of privacy that caused disturbing thoughts since the intruders were not previously present, not experienced, and only conjecturing while thinking they can judge morality when they are unconsciously attempting to judge what they cannot sense while disregarding firsthand sentiments, and therefore cannot sensibly judge, and then attempt to apply a Democratic vote count when a census gender count is in the other majority while their miscalculations and misrepresentations harmed with no significant benefits against a father providing significant benefits with harmless achievements that were privately and peaceably assembled under the U.S. First, Fourth, and Fourteenth Amendments.

When I lived in Statesville, N.C., and Statesville did not like my private rules containing significant benefits and successful achievements, I did not like their rules of no significant benefits and failure, and then I protested through the Fourteenth, First, Fourth, and Fifth U.S. Constitutional Amendments while not substantially harming others, and then I moved to another locale rather than submit to the socialist party of WWII Germany committing genocide against another culture.

There are usually two different groups of people, the superior that want to make others better by suggesting improvements, or the inferior that wanted to selfishly think they are better using one word or one comma after many pages of writ that they cannot mostly refute then attempt to bring the better down when the English language itself is not perfect, especially when continual editors of Dictionaries add more definitions after a linguistic becomes popular from a generation of vulgarization, or change a definition after etymology studies prior to controversies caused by

Shakespeare and the Church. A critic of Shakespeare stated let but a quibble and then Shakespeare would object. The best judgement is prudently agreeing to disagree as stated in my writing in the Federal District Court and refrain from publically stating what most might not comprehend. After considering several centuries, the better judgement has come from the Ten Commandments that can maintain tranquil ecology and success.

I do not write to get votes or make salacious profiteers more profitable, this is not a vulgar election with a mindless politician that has been brainwashed into stating what mob-rule wants to hear to get votes, this regards my real family that was created without a modern election, and if this writing does not help my family then this writing might help another family. One of my intellectual colleagues once told me before the millennium that he was raising his children with no television while he did Bible study with his children and his wife was home schooling. I recently called the foregoing colleague and asked for a reference and then asked how his children were doing, and he said that every child graduated from a respectable college and are now working respectable professions, and the foregoing is what would have happened for my children if there were not invasions of privacy. Expressing a variety of experiences should not be discriminated against while expressing variety is not as significant as individual merit.

Other than family and individual achievements that are respectable, and that worth does not necessarily mean monetary policy, since I earn only a 1/4 of what I earned in the past, although, I work a respectable profession in private security that secures the safety and rights of other families, businesses, private property, and public property against intruders, thieves, etc. .... In regards of decency, most men agree that a respectable woman dresses respectfully outside the home. If a woman takes her clothes off in front of her significant other in their home then that is acceptable, however, if a woman strips down in public then that is indecent. There is irony when representatives of the public stripped my daughter down in public and then ironically stated another was indecent when the elected representatives are what is vulgarly indecent. The reality is that most respectable men do not want a permanent relationship with a vulgar woman that seduces other men, and the excessive divorce rate influenced from Hollywood proves thereof. When my youngest daughter arrived after the first custody change, and then after my wife looked in my daughter's suitcase, she was disturbed by how her mother was dressing her, and the way her mother was dressing her was as a stripper. What is worse, is that my daughter was 10 years old at that time. Years later

after I purchased a respectable wardrobe for my

daughter that most girls her age wished they had, and

then after her mother stripped her down in public, my

daughter showed up in Court wearing skin tight

spandex while I gained favor from the Ad Litem

because he knew that her mother was teaching her to

seduce men rather than earn the respect of men.

Moreover, wearing such tawdry and skimpy clothes in

Court disrespects the decorum of the Court. After the

foregoing occurred, I wanted my sons away from my

youngest daughter while I fought for custody of my

sons. Since then, there continues to be lesser men out

there that do not care about a father raising respectable

sons that hopefully might choose respectable women. If

my daughters would remember the gifts that they gave

their father such as the eldest daughter giving a gift

stating: #1 Dad, and youngest daughter giving a gift

stating, "God gave me the best Dad", then the lesser objectors can be considered as in denial and are going to lose against the foregoing gifts while any change of thereof can be considered as brainwashing and coercing from mob-rule that use an illusion and their delusion from sleazy vulgar trash. As for the belated intruders, their vicarious feelings are not as significant as the feelings experienced in real time.

The scientific calculation is that siring gender balances can maintain equality and respect for trade in the population rather than women seducing men into brainwashing, coercing, stigmatizing, insulting, debauching, and then killing his fellow man. What was really going on behind the scenes is that my youngest son had what her mother referred to as a godfather, whom did not sire any children, however, he wanted to maintain a relationship with my youngest son and bankrolled the slanderous custody change. Then their mother's boyfriend was also in on the slanderous

custody change when he sired six girls and no boys,

and wanted my sons for either raising them as if they

were his sons or give them to his daughters while his

reckless disregard for rules of civil procedure in the

District Court of Dundalk, Maryland proved thereof

when he invalidated trade to get my sons by trashing

my daughter using popular public vulgarity and injustice

when he is lucky that I did not exercise the Second

Amendment that night after a well-regulated Maryland

Circuit, Supreme, and District Court had ruled in my

favor, and then after subjugated and suffering through

the N.C. Courts, if I could do this over again their

mother's boyfriend would have been dead that night,

mostly because my sons would have immediately

known there father is no joke, and learned that when

they become fathers in the future they should be just as

serious and immediate in their decision, however,

others would have spun a different story therefore the true and correct story will be written from their father. There was an inmate in jail that told me that a judge in North Carolina sounded similar to a pimp when he told the inmate: "these are my women", when the women were not closely related to him nor married to him while the quoted opinion is a comment that causes violence or divorce. Trade is recognized in the Bible whereas if a father wanted a woman for his sons, he traded with another father when the foregoing is the Jewish way while thereof is under the definition of 'marry'. Most modern parents cannot wait to get their teenagers out of their house while in my house we had fun as long as there was an equal measure of work and fun. At this juncture there has not been prejudice, however, after siring a gender balance and merited functional family, and then calculating the census gender imbalance and unmerited dysfunctional fatherless families, I cannot let others state prejudice while in denial of their prejudice. The reality is that junior was misled by others, and then ungratefully and publically attacked senior and then senior challenged junior.

After others brainwashed and coerced my youngest daughter, then moments after I won the custody hearing in Dundalk Maryland and walked outside, my youngest daughter was in a vehicle and I heard her kicking and screaming from fear after being told by others that her father was going to harm her and that is when I knew that others had abused my youngest daughter since one does not go from happy and joyful in her father's custody to kicking, screaming, and hating in her mother's custody after being abused by sleazy vulgar trash. Then months later after a slanderous Court hearing, I grieved because after improving junior and then others publically used junior to slander his father, his father did not want to put more public pressure on his thirteen year old son at that time since his father wanted his son succeeding in the future, therefore there was a dilemma and grief. After the last custody hearing my children came into my house to get their stuff, and I stated I love you, I love you, I love you for every one of my children and then my youngest son turned and looked at his father while junior wiped his tears with his forearm. After mob-rule charged, and then later junior matured as an adult, the time is now for confronting the Court and junior while Governments debate on ruling from a real few or the extrajudicial prejudice from the vicarious many. Candidly, others objections and invasion of privacy is from others sleazy vulgar trash without calculation from a census gender count nor consideration of a sired gender balance and merited functional family. I can ensure that the main circuit in question was absolutely completed and successful before mob-rule invaded privacy.

After recently speaking with a convenience store clerk, he stated what we want is a room full of women, and then I corrected him and stated what we want is a room from a man with a woman without others extraneously interfering. Then when the impotency of others did not sire any sons and then take his sons, their objections are from thieves trying to invalidate trade of which "the Laws of Nature and of Nature's God entitle them", Declaration of Independence 1776, when in a natural setting a mother is not strong enough to take his children, therefore, she has to rely on mob-rule to take his children and is why the police are no better than thieves that trespass and plunder when if the police go in his house and take his children then the police are criminals hiding behind a spurious badge when before the police took my children, I taught my children to respect the police, however, the Statesville, North Carolina police can be considered as thieves.

The issue with many mothers is they are only interested in what is modernly popular, and that was not a serious issue several decades ago when the Federal Communication Commission as an independent agency agreed with journalistic ethics and there were fewer television stations that avoided pandering to popular public vulgarity and sought mostly family programming while the broadcast was through the airwaves and the viewers did not pay since the profit was from business advertising. In modern times, there are many television stations competing for profit and they pander to salacious interests to profiteer and then broadcast popular public vulgarity. If a mother attempts to raise children today through the television, then the children become corrupt, and that is why my children were corrupted before and after my custody.

The issue with American police is that the police are from modern voters, and when voters become corrupt the police become corrupt and then make statements from popular public vulgarity. If others want to vote then they must realize that most fathers vote for their fellow father while every son is derived from their father and must respect his father and then after we acknowledge the foregoing we protest, and then when a woman miscalculates and disregards the foregoing into a degeneration then the founding documents of America need restating without votes from women since there were no women voters when the American founding documents were written, and then after women cause dysfunction then the founding documents again need restating.

It is not easy to maintain harmonious relations with every woman at the same time because that can involve psychoanalyzing each woman's menstrual cycle since the variations in her menstrual cycle can cause different emotional responses. Do not rewind and belatedly and vicariously question with a vernacular without considering emotional instabilities in a woman's prior menstrual cycle when after harsh questioning that can belatedly cause inharmonious and slanderous responses from inconsistencies between her prior menstrual cycle and current menstrual cycle, or when brainwashed, coerced, and/or public pressured from capricious vicissitudes with ulterior motives of others that can excessively entangle and extraneously interfere when her father psychoanalyzed ovulation of her menstrual cycle as the best time for harmonious relations, and then when others belatedly question something that happened in a relationship they need to understand that perhaps that was a premenstrual moment when worse is when my daughter used a premenstrual moment to state more slander.

In the aftermath with the same care first mentality I wrote a psychoanalytical perspective to help alieve the public pressure that caused denial in my daughter so that my daughter could again achieve, and then I wanted my daughter to attend college, then reunite and then write together and improve upon my prior writings referencing Sigmund and Anna Freud whom are also Jewish, and when that did not happen I had to continue writing alone from experience while considering male and female perspectives.

Men, intellectuals, and doctors prudently agree on privacy while agreeing to disagree rather than women voting with inconsistencies between their menstrual cycles, and then counting vacillating votes with capricious vicissitudes from unsteady women with weakness or jealousy that only consider couples for sleazy vulgar gossiping trash. If others do not want to ask her father for her hand in marriage then marry her rather than publically debauch her. I met the fathers of every long term woman I dated except one since she did not know her father while she caused the most trouble and grief.

I can calculate the surplus from the census gender count and achieve more peace than political voters advocating invasion of privacy with extraneous rhetoric that ostracize from tyranny of the majority while in denial of being salacious thieves and in denial of the reality that really exists in the modern population. I already considered tyranny of the majority when father as the first vote wanted detachment from daughter and then daughter calls mother and asks her mother for her father to spend more time with her, and then mother calls father and asks father to spend more time with daughter. If at that time I talked with my sons and told them their mother wanted their father to spend more time with their sister, meaning I would spend less time with them, then my sons would state no, therefore the votes from my sons would be two and three. If at that time I believed that majority rules on private property then I would have afflicted tyranny of the majority against my daughter when their father made the decision to maintain the minority vote of two from mother and daughter as a secret from my sons and spend equal time with daughter and sons while finding a way to keep improving my sons while the improvement continued until spurious public politicians wanted invasions of privacy with majority vote counts and ostracizing from tyranny of the majority. Since I was against tyranny of the majority when I made the foregoing decision, then I will always be against tyranny of the majority since majority rule might rule most of the time on public property, however, majority rule does not rule every time in a refuge on private property, and I am sure if Thomas Jefferson and James Madison were alive they would agree. Moreover, the reality in modern America is that most women have lost their virginity and have been with multiple men before marrying; therefore, why would a modern father be scrutinized for giving his daughter experience while securing her virginity before being with another while the boy who takes her virginity and does not marry her is not scrutinized? If most modern American women had no experience before marrying and stayed married until death do they part, and there were the same amount of women as men in the region, then I could understand some objections, however, that is not the case in modern America, therefore, Americans are in denial of their double standard then trying to compel a father to forget about his family after some prefer women with no experience to make it easier for them to debauch his daughter when her father did not want her to be like her mother, and when others ask who do you love, the word love has multiple meanings when love is first stated among family members and then later from couples while others must not forget there was relativeness, achievements, upper hand and signatures from sons. The issue with mob-rule is others invade privacy and then waste time against the superior, supreme, and superior. Then after others question signatures, the belated questioning from spurious imposters is not significant.

After my religious writing and being charged then attending the last custody hearing, I heard their mother mumble that she forgot about her persuasive call while others interfered in the middle of father and mother when while their mother made that persuasive call, she failed to make the next call before others intruded while peddling lies, hatred, and distrust in pursuit of personal political gain. Sending adult men to jail as if they are children sent to their room is ineffective since most criminals repeat crime and return to jail. Many criminals only need discipline and counseling from their father when raised by their father, and raised with good friends for caring for his fellow man.

I write from firsthand knowledge and instrument on paper through family and the 4-H from head, heart, hands, and health rather than through hackers, cynics, critics, and thieves that cannot agree to disagree while an immediate decision is expected from the Federal Fourth Circuit Court. The U.S Supreme Court already agrees with privacy when if I want I can narrow the right of privacy from an absolute, although, I prefer securing privacy for many when I can make many look foolish after many have wasted time and money invading privacy without answering my complaint. The people that elect politicians that follow thereof cannot balance what they sire nor the budget.

The Court should consider what we have in common with our U.S. Constitutional Rights and International Human Rights rather than what is in common with spurious modern politicians that invade privacy, disregard families, achievements, and then invalidate trade while degenerating the population. The spurious modern politicians do not understand family nor humanity when only relying on salacious profiteering from misleading political games to entertain the crowd of intruders and then gather majority votes to ostracize while debauching his daughter and taking his sons to continue their degenerative stack. After others invaded privacy and the fatherland causing divisions, what I appreciate the most are similar encouragements with accompaniments after I believed in my family rather than belatedly discriminated against with political persecutions when thereof does not relate to only the New Testament that is mostly about unrelated families when the New Testament is nothing more than

intruders asking for forgiveness after trespassing when

the word trespassing is in the so called Lord's prayer

since the New Testament advises that followers go into

another's house and if the homeowner does not let

them in, then the Christians stigmatize the homeowner

with extraneous rhetoric. When a Government models

their authority from the New Testament they also

become spurious imposters and thieves while

disregarding the Old Testament that is mostly about

related families.

After there was poetic form in my family, the

worse is when degenerates conjectured on nature and

then questioned the author while wasting another's time

when a sired gender balance and merited functional

family wins over unmerited dysfunction from sleazy

vulgar gossiping trash where the unskilled salaciously

profiteer from degenerative strippers while I presented

poetry from my daughter when father and daughter exchanged profound and prolific writings, and then after others intruded, she stated "he loved me", and then said his letters are in the top left drawer of her dresser. Why would mob-rule argue for a judge to issue a warrant to invade her father's home to search for love followed by a female hiding behind a spurious badge knocking on her father's door, and then after answered she showed a search warrant to search for love and then later asking to search the top left dresser drawer for love letters in my house with reckless disregard for the Fourth Amendment of the U.S. Constitution. What the female hiding behind a spurious badge did not know is that before my daughter was brainwashed and coerced by others, she respected privacy and hid some letters in the back of her drawer and left only the letter she did not mind others reading in the front of her drawer, and that letter is only what the police discovered and confiscated.

Statesville North Carolina is a City of no respect for family, nor achievements, nor real love, nor fun. The aftermath of others was about put your hands up and step away from the poetry because they wanted my sons to run the next inner-city strip club. After others invaded privacy they must answer the burdens. I could have given away my U.S. citizenship like the 1000 people that yearly give away their U.S. citizenship and moved my family to another Country while there would still be more than a five million women surplus in the U.S. Those that invade privacy to profiteer by dramatically entertaining others followed by gambling and profiteering use a flimsy excuse thinking they are leveling the playing field, when their argument is not significant and unsubstantial when the census gender count is not equal while the only way there is equality regarding couples is if siring an equal amount of both genders; therefore, siring considerations that respect trade are more substantial than playing insincere confidence games to entertain others while intruding and counting votes from impotent and degenerative intruders with hateful and harmful ostracizing. The foregoing has wasted time rather than securing a sired gender balance and merited functional family with virtue and dignity while not extraneously under the color of law per 42 U.S.C §1983 and §1985.

At times I can support one way, a few way, or many way when self-evident men already agreed on separate stations and then formed separate executive, judicial, and congressional perspectives while modern American men have no excuse for not agreeing to disagree when self-evident men had already agreed to disagree, and then when questioned, separation with private property was further acknowledged in U.S.

Constitutional Rights, and then after others question

which perspective I support, I support multiple

perspectives that respect privacy and head for the light

without voting for tyranny of the majority. As for the

modern American media, I dare them to mention my

name without my consent in a derogatory way after I

already filed a lawsuit against a City while supporting

United States Constitutional Rights when if higher

Courts reject my complaint, then like I moved to another

State, I will move to another Country while supporting

only International Human Rights and publishing most of

herein while telling the truth about how modern

American women run a confidence game on men

where a woman seduces a wealthy man, have his

children, seduce other men, and then go to Democratic

Courts and take his children and his earned wealth, and

is why I no longer date modern American women when

if thereof is published then thereof will cause more

terrorism because most terrorism is because the United States is meddling in the affairs of other Countries, then after foreigners watch American television they do not like the sleazy vulgarity and do not want the sleazy vulgar American influence brainwashing his wife and his children. There are Countries where Courts execute an adulteress or the mother's boyfriend immediately, and now readers know why. I advise negotiate before it is too late, therefore the choice is either respect a United States Citizen and his family then negotiate or assassinate a United States Citizen before the unrelated, insensible, and insensitive attempt to conquer absolute computations that contained nature with improvements that mob-rule tried to take over after "Democracy comes into being, after the poor have conquered their opponents, slaughtering some and banishing the rest."

As for their mother, what has she accomplished? Nothing except pander to a crowd of intruders while forgetting their father then attempting to disgrace their father and humanity, then when others think strength is joining her treachery then their father will consider pulling out not only a gun, a tactical machine gun. As for the opposition, do not compel me to break out the real calculator when their opposition will lose from their miscalculations and unrelated beliefs that dishearten followed by broadcasting my heart and love to others and while that broadcast might sound good to others, after others followed her slanderous misrepresentation and ironically think I broke her heart, the truth is she ganged with mob-rule and broke my stronger heart and then estranged as a prostitute to entertain mob-rule. I will and can grieve when considering sentiments that included my sons when I expected my children to return from free will without others excessively entangling and extraneously interfering. After others excessively entangled, extraneously interfered, and invaded privacy, the following thoughts came naturally:

1. Get a 45 caliber and then shoot the mother's boyfriend in the head.

2. Attach explosives to the Iredell County North Carolina Department of Social Services.

3. Get a machine gun and then walk into the incompetent Statesville, North Carolina Court and then machine gun them down.

4. Get a 44 magnum and then walk into the social psychologist office and then shoot the degenerative social psychologist whom pandered in the head.

What others do not understand is that their unnatural invasions of privacy is what caused those natural thoughts. Others are lucky I have self-control, can self-govern, and there is a grievance process in the

U.S. Constitutional First Amendment while a Government of subjugation had to follow me for fear that I might execute one or two of the items or every item on the foregoing list. Others cannot follow every father for the rest of their life, therefore, I advise restrain and refrain from invading a real father's privacy or the foregoing list will be reconsidered by another father in the future.

Several decades ago there were no mass shootings, and that is when America was great, now there are mass shootings every year while the larger the City the more shootings. Something is wrong in modern America and taking guns away is not going to solve the problem when there is information on the internet for another to manufacture a gun at home or create explosives then instead of shooting one or two with a gun, the explosives will kill many. The answers to the modern problems are in this document.

Regardless of how a relationship was started, if I went with all men are created equal and the female was happy before an invasion and heartless disruption then every man agrees with one another and states she is wrong when I can scientifically calculate the foregoing with a sired gender balance and merited functional family and state that others are insensibly, insensitively, and unscientifically, wrong. Remember the foregoing since no objection can sensibly, sensitively, and scientifically object. This is no game since I can win either a tennis match or science while others wasted my time with others profiteering by playing controversial games. Some stated this is a perfect storm after there was excellence and perfection before others intruded that then caused the storm.

Consider two fathers that sired a gender balance, are friends, and barter with one another while father 'A' can build and repair anything and father 'B' can hunt and fish everything while mother 'A' can cook anything and mother 'B' can sew everything while their families have gardens, are neighbors and are mostly self-sufficient, healthy, happy, and raised harmlessly with minimal media exposure while their children are friends with one another, and then a politician knocks on their door and says that the country nor continent was attacked but they want their children to kill others on the other side of the world because most voters are not as self-sufficient as the foregoing families while politicians invalidate rights and invade privacy then pander to voter interests and create tyranny of the majority policies for most voters to remain in power, and then to maintain voter interest in their political party, politicians need the media that influence the votes of mob-rule that want to be entertained with profiteering and pandering to controversies from politicians that compete over different ideologies with voter interests, and over resources to protect the businesses whom trade in other countries and layoff locals.

What would be a family's natural response from the foregoing, and what would the families say to one another? Why does a Government need to invade the privacy of successful citizens? Why is there over a five million women surplus? Why are there more fatherless homes in the City? Why are there excessive inner-city street killings in America? Why are there mass killings in America? Why did men get together in another Country and then decide to fly planes in the World Trade Center? Why is not America finding alternative energies for less dependence on foreign oil? Why does America sign free trade agreements with other Countries and let businesses move jobs to another Country? Why does a Country with only 5 percent of the world's population need the most powerful military to defend the 5 percent? Why would 5 percent of the population pay more than 70 percent of the military

expenditures to defend other countries? Why is the

Country in nearly 20 trillion dollars in debt? Why does

not the United Nations with a coalition force defend

other Countries rather than mostly Americans? Why

would a woman from the establishment be considered

for President of the United States when there is more of

the foregoing status quo? I hear the broadcasted music

when no one will ever care and love more than her

biological father when if compelled her biological father

can match the minimal care and love from unrelated

others while her biological father hoped that she would

respect and appreciate her biological father's care and

love and then eventually find another that could at least

care and love while hoping his sons would learn care

and love without others hopelessly, heartlessly, and

hatefully invading privacy while ganging with mob-rule

then genocide closer genetics that cared and loved

from a biological father's sired gender balance and
merited functional family. The worse is when others
belatedly attempt to take credit when lowering with a
low and left after what was already high, low and high
from a right, left and right.

APPENDIX IV

UNPUBLISHED

UNITED STATES COURT OF APPEALS
FOR THE FOURTH CIRCUIT

No. 16-1549

DAVID THOMAS SILVERS SR.,

Plaintiff – Appellant,

v.

IREDELL COUNTY DEPARTMENT OF SOCIAL

SERVICES; DONALD C. WALL, D.S.S Dir., in

individual and official capacities; PAXTON BUTLER,

Asst. D.A., in individual and official capacities; CITY OF

STATESVILLE,

Defendants – Appellees.

Appeal from the United States District Court for the Western District of North Carolina, at Statesville. Richard L. Voorhees,

---

Submitted: October 13th, 2016

Decided: October 17th, 2016

Before Niemeyer, Duncan, and WYNN, Circuit Judges.

Affirmed by unpublished per curiam opinion.

David Thomas Silvers, Sr., Appellant Pro Se. Patrick Houghton Flanagan, CRANFILL, SUMNER & HARTZOG, LLP, Charlotte, North Carolina; James R. Morgan, Jr., WOMBLE CARLYLE SANDRIDGE & RICE, PLLC, Winston-Salem, North Carolina, for Appellees.

Unpublished opinions are not binding precedent in this circuit.

PER CURIAM:

David Thomas Silvers, Sr., appeals the district court's orders denying relief on his civil complaint. We have reviewed the record and find no reversible error. Accordingly, we affirm for the reasons stated by the district court. Silvers v. Iredell Cty. DSS, No. 5:15-cv-00083-RLV-DCK (W.D.N.C. Feb. 3, 2016 & Apr. 15, 2016). We dispense with oral arguments because the facts and legal contentions are adequately presented in the materials before this court and argument would not aid the decisional process.

AFFIRMED

APPENDIX V

The most disturbing aspect of invasions of privacy is that the public tries to execute another whether physically or metaphysically when literally or figuratively dismissing the real justice of the peace that secures unalienable rights such as right of privacy that prevents the belatedly inexperienced from conjecturing and then speculating about what they did not experience.

Email to youngest daughter on 11/07/2016 prior to mailing writ on Election Day of November 8, 2016.

"… *What you need to understand is that my sons were an integral part of the ethos in the immediate family while slandering under oath is not a moral nature nor a guiding belief of any scrupulous citizen and while I gave you a choice the night before you left to return or not, and you promised to return, my minimum expectation was for my younger sons returning so that I could continue improving them and when that did not happen, you failed. You were supposed to be the one that when you and my sons visited their mother you would defend your father and mitigate the yearly hostilities from you mother and ensure my sons return. The reality is that I do not want a woman doing to my sons what your mother and you did to me, such as broken promises and smearing while disregarding the success in the family, therefore, most of this continued legal fight is about merited functional families, my sons, and mankind. [My expectations of you now are the same expectations I had when visiting your mother in 2004 (note: this last sentence was paraphrased).]"*

PRE AND POST ELECTION NOTES: On the day of the 2016 election I mentioned a Constitutional Amendment should be considered whereas whomever won the most States should automatically be the Vice President and could be President if also gaining the most votes in the Electoral College when the foregoing was regarding the 2012 election where I believed that after Mitt Romney - of whom I rejected after he publically attacked Trump and the character of a man he never met - won the most States in 2012, he should have been the Vice President and Obama President since Obama won the

Electoral College, and how thereof could minimize

excessive divisiveness in the Country since when there

is not a moderate position, opposing parties can at

times lead to moderation of future policies, and that is

why the two party system can at times be useful if they

worked together rather than against one another, when

if they worked together they could accomplish better

than either party could accomplish by themselves. For

the most part the framers of the Constitution were bright

enough to understand the need for the Electoral

College that prevents only a few States with densely

populated areas of mob-rule from electing a President.

Regarding the 2016 election, since Donald Trump won

the most States and the Electoral College, then the

Democrats should not be complaining and protesting

from only densely populated areas of mob-rule,

especially when their excess of popular votes is only .2

percent. If most States need candidate 'A' over

candidate 'B', then the few States for candidate 'B'

should work with their State Governors to reconcile the

differences in and between States rather than burden a

President-elect from only a handful of States. Since

most of the 2016 objections against candidate 'A' from

the densely populated Cities regard immigration then

the States on the immigration borders need

considering, and while California was for candidate 'B'

and has an immigration border, then if California wants

to open their border and give immigrants residency in

their State then that is what should be permitted,

however, since Texas, Florida, and Arizona are for

candidate 'A', then other States have no excuse since

their Governors will not be able to persuade others

against Texas, Florida, and Arizona immigration

policies supported by the President-Elect.

The Democrats mostly rely on inner-city votes

while the people that are belatedly protesting are in the

Cities where their economies are in banking, finance, insurance, printing, publishing, and entertainment when a country cannot be self-sufficient when only relying on the foregoing. It as if the people in the Cities are in a bubble and do not know what surrounds them when there was a time when the rural economy was where the money flowed into the Cities and now the money flows from outside the Country into the Cities and while there is minimal change on the Cities there are major changes on the rural parts of the Country and that is why Donald Trump won the election while their belated personal attacks from the Cities did not overcome the electorate followed by their unacceptable destruction of public property that only proves that their urban influences on the Country are degenerative. Donald Trump has already rescinded the banishing of resident Muslims while what Donald Trump needs to state is that whomever was in the Country on the date of election will be considered in regards of, and without, separating parents and children, although, he must also state that future immigration policy needs tightening to prevent immigrants from coming over the border then accepted after propagation while taking jobs away from citizens. What Donald Trump and I realized after working with citizens in the construction industry is that Americans are complaining that their bids are being undercut by crews of Mexicans whereas many Mexicans live under the same roof and can afford to work at lower billing rates while much of the money is going back to Mexico where the American dollar is stronger than the Peso. Manufacturing jobs also need consideration whereas free trade agreements compelled American businesses to hire people in other countries to manufacture goods to remain competitive while neglecting fellow citizens.

A few decades ago, when Wal-Mart was attempting to take over market share from K-Mart, Wal-Mart advertised their products were "made in America", and then many consumers switched to Wal-Mart, and now that Wal-Mart is selling mostly foreign products, there needs to be another campaign for "made in America", and that is why Trump was elected. I had always thought what needs to happen is a President needs to meet at least yearly with the most influential business leaders in a conference with the objective of keeping jobs from leaving the Country by leveraging tariffs if business leaders cannot come to an agreement on their duty as a citizen to employ most of their people in the Country. The reason for the meetings is because if tariffs are immediately enacted without considering business operations, then some businesses will fail if they do not have an adequate opportunity and time to prepare for bringing jobs back in the Country.

I recall considering the foregoing a decade ago when writing: "oh the irony, so much irony" after belated intruders attempted to think I was in their bubble when they were in a bubble that lost the 2016 election.

After my youngest daughter experienced her father as a real man then after others belatedly coerced her into congressional demands of what they think a father should be, she needs to realize that the majority are with sons of a bitch that have only led to census gender imbalances and unmerited dysfunctional fatherless families when potent fathers from sired gender balances and merited functional families are the ones that will and can determine peaceful relations.

Honestly and candidly I reject others invasions of privacy that try to compel me into considering a competition of whom should run the Country rather than considering what was already more merit and love than the vulgar commoners that wasted my family and time.

I recall a couple of years into the aftermath that some in Hollywood wanted me to become a celebrity, and went as far as taping personal relations I had at that time with my girlfriend in my house while trying to convince me into a reality show without my consent.

After many women only chase celebrity status, the fame from thereof does not determine a man's true character since if a woman only wants his fame and if his fame fades then she might leave him, and is why I have mostly rejected celebrity status when I knew if I was single and not a celebrity then I had a better chance of discovering true love since I would rather be single than be used by a heartless woman pursuing only what others thought of a character when most are misleading into lusting for aesthetics, passion, or fame that cannot sustain, and is why there are more divorces in Hollywood than anywhere else in the Country.

After I rejected others invasions of privacy and their attempt at a reality show to entertain others while profiteering, those that invaded privacy stated that the Patriot Act signed after 9/11 voided the Fourteenth, Fourth, and Fifth Amendments of the U.S. Constitution, and that is when I decided to challenge thereof and found myself in the middle of multiple groups of people, those in the entertainment industry that did not want privacy and those assisting me with privacy while that digressed into controversies in and between father and mother, or couples, or father and daughter, or father and son(s), and what is success when there was no need for controversy when there were peaceful relations with everyone in my sired family, every former spouse, my family I grew up in, and everyone in the community, and is why on June 5th, 2004 I patted myself on the back, and then intruders became home wreckers that treacherously caused havoc.

APPENDIX VI

The following genealogical research was from my Aunt Rachel whom stated years earlier that our Jewish lineage left Germany more than 200 years ago and resided in the Appalachian mountains of N.C., then my grandfather like Moses came down from the mountain with the 10 Commandments into Georgia and sired a dozen children with a perfect gender balance of 6 boys and 6 girls, then after Athens Georgia interfered he left during a time when popular public opinion was trending with a theory from "leading scientists, politicians, and celebrities around the world. Research was funded by distinguished philanthropies, and carried out at prestigious universities. The crisis is reported frequently in the media. The science is taught in college and high school classrooms. Its supporters included Theodore Roosevelt, Woodrow Wilson, and Winston Churchill. It was approved by Supreme Court justices

Oliver Wendell Holmes and Louis Brandeis, who ruled in its favor. The famous names who supported it included Alexander Graham Bell, inventor of the telephone; activist Margaret Sanger; botanist Luther Burbank; Leland Stanford, founder of Stanford University; the novelist H.G. Wells; the playwright George Bernard Shaw; and hundreds of others. Nobel Prize winners gave support. Research was backed by the Carnegie and Rockefeller Foundations. The Cold Springs Harbor Institute was built to carry out this research, but important work was also done at Harvard, Yale, Princeton, Stanford, and Johns Hopkins. Legislation to address the crisis was passed in states from New York to California. These efforts had the support of the National Academy of Sciences, the American Medical Association, and the National Research Council. It was said that if Jesus were alive, he would have supported this effort. All in all, the research, legislation, and molding of public opinion

surrounding the theory went on for almost a half a

century. Those who opposed the theory were shouted

down and called reactionary, blind to reality, or just

plain ignorant. But in hindsight, what is surprising is that

so few people objected. Today, we know that this

famous theory that gained so much support was

actually pseudoscience. The crisis it claimed was

nonexistent. And the actions taken in the name of this

theory were morally and criminally wrong. Ultimately,

they led to the deaths of millions of people. The theory

was eugenics, and its history is so dreadful - and, to

those who were caught up in it, so embarrassing – that

it is now rarely discussed. But it is a story that should

be well known to every citizen, so that its horrors are

not repeated. The theory of eugenics postulated a crisis

of the gene pool leading to the deterioration of the

human race. The best human beings were not breeding

as rapidly as the inferior ones" while at that time the inferior ones were stated to be "foreigners, immigrants, Jews, degenerates, the unfit, and the 'feeble minded'. [When aforementioned statements are mostly from an Athenian majority with invidious discrimination against the minority, since whenever civilization ironically degenerates from popular public opinion, the real superiority are from the Jewish that rescued civilization with the 10 Commandments, and technology built that Albert Einstein considered when I uphold thereof.] "Francis Galton", a respected British scientist, first speculated about this area, but his ideas were taken far beyond anything he intended. They were adopted by science-minded Americans, as well as those who had no interest in science but who were worried about the immigration of inferior races early in the twentieth century – 'dangerous human pests' who represented 'the rising tide of imbeciles' and who were polluting the best of the human race. The eugenicists and [those opposed to immigration] joined forces to put a stop to this. The plan was to identify individuals who were feeble-minded – [at that time it was stated that] Jews were agreed to be largely feeble-minded, but so were many foreigners, as well as blacks – and stop them from breeding by isolation in institutions or by sterilization. As Margaret Sanger said, 'Fostering the good-for-nothing at the expense of the good is an extreme cruelty … there is no greater curse to posterity than that of bequeathing them an increasing population of imbeciles' She spoke of the burden of caring for 'this dead weight of human waste'. Such views were widely shared. H.G. Wells spoke against 'ill-trained swarms of inferior citizens'. Theodore Roosevelt said that "Society has no business to permit degenerates to reproduce their kind". Luther Burbank: 'Stop permitting criminals and weaklings to reproduce'. George Bernard Shaw said that only eugenics could save mankind. There was

overt racism in this movement, exemplified by texts

such as 'The Rising Tide of Color against White World

Supremacy', by American author Lothrop Stoddard.

But, at the time, racism was considered an

unremarkable aspect of the effort to attain a marvelous

goal – the improvement of humankind in the future. It

was this avant-garde notion that attracted the most

liberal and progressive minds of a generation. California

was one of the twenty-nine American states to pass

laws allowing sterilization, but it proved the most

forward-looking and enthusiastic – more sterilizations

were carried out in California than anywhere in

America. Eugenics research was funded by the

Rockefeller Foundation. The latter was so enthusiastic

that even after the center of the eugenics effort moved

to Germany, and involved the gassing of individuals

from mental institutions, the Rockefeller Foundation

continued to finance German researchers at a very high level. (The foundation was quit about it, but they were still funding research in 1939, only months before the onset of World War II.) Since the 1920's, American eugenicists had been jealous because the Germans had taken leadership of the movement away from them. The Germans were admirably progressive. They set up ordinary-looking houses where 'mental defectives' were brought and interviewed one at a time, before being led into a back room, which was, in fact, a gas chamber. There, they were gassed with carbon monoxide, and their bodies disposed of in a crematorium located on the property. Eventually, this program was expanded into a vast network of concentration camps located near railroad lines, enabling the efficient transport and killing of ten million undesirables. After World War II, nobody was a eugenicist, and nobody had ever been a eugenicist. Biographers of the celebrated and the powerful did not dwell on the attractions of this philosophy to their subjects, and sometimes did not mention it at all. Eugenics ceased to be a subject for college classrooms, although some argue that its ideas continue to have currency in disguised form. But in retrospect, three points stand out. First, despite the construction of Cold Springs Harbor Laboratory, despite the efforts at universities and the pleadings of lawyers, there was no scientific basis for eugenics. In fact, nobody at that time knew what a gene really was. The movement was able to proceed because it employed vague terms never rigorously defined. 'Feeble-mindedness' could mean anything from poverty and illiteracy to epilepsy. Similarly, there was no clear definition of 'degenerate' or 'unfit'. Second, the eugenics movement was really a social program masquerading as a scientific one. What drove it was concern about immigration, and racism and undesirable people moving into one's neighborhood or country. Once again, vague terminology helped conceal what was really going on. Third, and most distressing, the scientific establishment in both the United States and Germany did not mount any sustained protest. Quite the contrary. In Germany, scientists quickly fell into line with the program. Modern German researchers have gone back to review Nazi documents from the 1930's. They expected to find directives telling scientists what research should be done. But none were necessary. In the words of Ute Deichman, 'Scientists, including those who were not members of the Nazi party, helped to get funding for their work through their modified behavior and direct cooperation with the State' Deichman speaks of the 'active role of scientists themselves in regard to Nazi race policy … where research was aimed at confirming the racial doctrine … no external pressure can be documented' German scientists adjusted their research interests to the new policies. And those few who did not adjust disappeared." - Michael Crichton from the Appendix in his 2004 book: "State of Fear".

My father enlisted in the Air Force then moved to Maryland, then before my Aunt passed away, of which was more than a year after my immediate family was disrupted and after I had already upheld the 10 Commandments in my private religious patristic writing, my Aunt left her Bible open on the 10 Commandments for the family while at the funeral my father directed my attention to an infant of a cousin as if to say, do not worry about your sons, the lineage will continue without them while my thoughts were losing my sons to sleazy gossiping trash was not acceptable and now the grievance continues in the Court system. While I was growing up I had a step-sister and we went to a Baptist Church while my neighbors on one side attended a Catholic Church and on the other side attended a

Synagogue while everyone was friendly and peacefully living among one another while separated by private property and different religions. When others think they know the inner-city streets, I have also been there and done that, and won the inner-city way of physically knocking my girlfriend's ex-boyfriend out on Pratt Street in Baltimore City. At that time my girlfriend was also the mother of two unrestrained young children while the ex-boyfriend was the father of the young children, although, their father was not living in the house while my girlfriend was letting her mother and step-father - whom was also the father of the ex-boyfriend - run over and depress my girlfriend using unrestrained children, similar to how my youngest daughter was depressed by her mother. I had already physically dominated as a rough sea of mob-rule, and then after siring children while their mother continued believing in the inner-city way of men physically fighting one another to win the girl while risking the well-being of one another, and then after refining sired children followed by signatures from my sons, then thereof is the better way. Mob-rule did not know what I experienced in my life and then after grieving in Court, mob-rule did not think I was physically tough enough to make it through jail, and then after many wins or draws in fights, although in self-defense, the State psychologist stated if I was in any more fights in jail they would use it against me. Later, an inmate took a swipe at me while I did nothing, because the State psychologists would have continued to force harmful drugs by stating that I was aggressive while word got around the inmates of me not fighting in self-defense then thinking I was less of a man when the inmates did not know about the coercive threat by the State psychologist while the jailers conspired and put the man whom took a swipe at me back in the section of the jail that I was in to see what would happen when I was ready to physically knock him out if he tried to take another swipe at me, regardless of what that inner-city Court system with voters of mob-rule stated since the adversarial Court system is similar to mob-rule whereas instead of physically fighting one another they mentally fight to win the girl, when this is not about a girl, this is about families and individuals getting along and being friendly with one another and when they disagree, they agree to disagree, and then when all else fails, secure private property and maintain separation of powers. The inmate whom took a swipe at me, did not test me again while we got along without a fight. The public Court system plays too many harmful games and they are lucky that no one was killed because if I had to do this over again, I would not let a lawyer get in the middle of their biological father and their mother's boyfriend, and the reason I let that happen was because I had been teaching my sons civilly rather than barbarically, although, after I discovered that not all bar associations are civil, violence can be a consequence of their negligence, injustice, and incivility.

CONCLUSION

Others have no excuse whereas I am genetically strong with dexterity, a sired gender balance, and merited functional family with skilled mental aptitude that was skillfully proven with published code in the Amended Complaint while I am not the perpetrator that invaded privacy and did not follow rules of civil procedure then personally and publically attacked, when prior to invasions of privacy, I considered others outside my family and was proud of my sired children while not flaunting my ability before others attacked, although, when considering self-defense, and if not for family, for self-defense, and then when challenged I will prove that those that invaded privacy and attacked are crooked and are the immoral and inferior degenerates.

The amicable, amiable, and affable way forms the best way while respectfully asking her father for her hand in marriage rather than physically fighting one another on the inner-city streets, or mentally fighting with physical inferences in an adversarial Court system of negligence and injustice. My eldest daughter and her boyfriend agreed with merit and sincere sentiments while intruders should have asked for my youngest daughter's hand in marriage rather than others teaching sleazy vulgar trash when my sons should have returned in their father's custody while their father continued representing virtue. There are hundreds of murders every year in the most populated cities while others are lucky I waited for others to consider virtue, merit, and charity when if there is no justice I advise executing the spurious imposter immediately while referencing this writing when this writing counters all belated objections.

The Rainbow of Promise

On 11/14/16 I observed a double ended rainbow off the Virginia coast with an arch hidden in the clouds, and while I am a true believer that one must work with nature to achieve the best results, like some Romans, I had technically considered a census gender count with a keystone at the center that would strengthen the arch for building a waterway with others while at the same time if my eldest daughter and sons are neglected I will not forgive their negligence after a rainbow of promise that supported my daughter and covered my sons. How did the aftermath followed by these writings begin? The aftermath was after I mailed a postcard to my daughter that pictured a rainbow that others thought a father should not send his daughter, followed by conjecture, harsh inquisition, and despair from a victimless and tumultuous pillow fight from an intruding Gladiator forum of mob-rule with goons, clowns, and jokers.

Like I wrote in the Informal Brief: "when what the plaintiff said and what the plaintiff did was mostly in response to what the plaintiff's daughter said or did in order to maintain domestic tranquility and her scholastic achievements", when the closeness was usually after someone outside the home depressed my daughter.

When my daughter had communicated on the phone with her mother twice a week every week while in my custody and visited her mother in another State during spring break two months before she left for the summer, and the only time my daughter complained to her mother was when her father was not spending enough time with her, then later visits her mother during the summer and after receiving a post card followed by vulgar commoners ironically stating abuse that they afflicted, then another can conclude that the vulgar commoners of mob-rule are in denial of advocating a gang of degenerates and crowd of intruders.

During my religious patristic writing, I met a woman that could have been influenced by that writing, although, I never asked her if she knew anything about that writing. She was the best woman I ever met in North Carolina whereas her father was a Dentist and owned his own Dentist business, and her mother was a former Miss. South Carolina, although, I had never put much faith in pompous pageants while their daughter was a Deacon at a Church, had graduated at the University of North Carolina with honors, and was a school teacher, like my last wife was at one time. She was about 12 years younger than me, and her dating protocol was for me to meet her Church group, her school faculty, her formal dance group, and then her father and mother. Since her five year College reunion was that year, I also met her Alumni. Every group approved of me and I spent Christmas holidays with her family while her family was close and she even danced

with father in the house while I also met her neighbor
and we went over to their neighbors house during the
holidays, then one night when I was close with her, she
told me she was still a virgin, and that is when I decided
marriage or nothing. I was not insensitive and perverted
as to ask her if she masturbated or how close her prior
relationships were like the socialists of antagonism that
think raising children is from a factory line or pod and
then questioned my daughter when if the sanctity of my
girlfriend's virginity was good enough for me then the
sanctity of my daughter's virginity was good enough for
others. I recall one night when my youngest daughter
was dressed in sheer and went outside in my driveway
in front of my truck knowing I was in my truck, and I told
her to cover up while the difference between a father
and mob-rule is that a father tells his daughter to cover
up while mob-rule advocates stripping her down while
in denial of their degenerative perversions when the

result of others insensitively and inappropriately asking her intimate questions was her later stripping down with lewd pictures of herself on the internet, of which a respectable man would have nothing to do with such a woman while my eldest daughter stated her sister was a prostitute. If it was not for being in the middle of legal proceedings at that time regarding my children, I would have married my girlfriend, and while she was willing to go through those legal proceedings with me, I did not want to burden such a good woman with what was at that time ungrateful children, especially since my last wife had previously stated: "You chose your children over me and look what they did to you", when at that time I stated it was what their mother did to my children. The reality is that the reason I chose my children over my last wife was because my last wife and my youngest daughter were contentiously struggling for my attention and disturbing the peace while my sons were observing and did not understand what was going on when I did not want my sons subjected to hostility in the home, and since my children had been improving, I decided that I could build a more tranquil and successful family structure with my virgin daughter and my sons, and that is what were the results until the totalitarian socialists of antagonism think that raising children should be from only one type of factory line or pod - when what they thought was their factory line or pod disregarded a five million women surplus with tolerance thereof - and then harshly questioned my youngest daughter and took my sons with tumultuous conjecture, slander, and hearsay.

And then after I wrote psychoanalytical and philosophical perspectives, I met another woman whom was part of the Mensa organization followed by more invasions of privacy from not only Government entities, invasions of privacy from Hollywood. The foregoing was very disturbing while I dated that girlfriend longer than I wanted in order to discover the truth of what she was hiding from me. At first it seemed she was assisting me in proceedings when she suggested I had women to the left of me and women to the right then asking what are my tactical or strategic thoughts about the case. What I gleaned was she was vicariously from a conspiracy for discovery when I knew she was not telling me the truth after her walls were covered with pictures from Japan while others were conjecturing and thinking I was trying to become an Emperor like in Japan, or in Rome with Caesar, and then after finding her bookshelf with Nazi publications then her asking me what book I preferred, and since I already read religion, Plato, and Aristotle, I chose Shakespeare. After questioning her, I discovered some were using me as a subject for gambling, then after I rejected her ideology, I allege she drugged me, then I camped in the mountains and thought for myself rather than what intruders wanted me to think while many followed me. The most disturbing scene in the mountains were actors trying to scare me into thinking the Nazis were coming. For the most part, most were assisting me while some attempted to influence me into religious or secular, father or mother, son or daughter, or Republican or Democratic controversies when I was only waiting for substantive due process while the Court was enslaving me into the locale and then depriving me due process for more than seven years. What I did not want is another living through the foregoing tumultuous experience, therefore, I remain a staunch advocate for the right of privacy, and the U.S. Second Amendment.

Like I wrote my father from due respect, I respected his line item veto in Appendix VI when it was the mistakes of coercive intruders after June 5th 2004 that caused distress in the well-being of his son and well-being of my children, when prior to their mistakes I worked in a reputable profession, was a homeowner, and everyone in my immediate family was healthy, happy, and successful while harmless to others. The vulgar commoners thought that my children should publish something about their family without respecting their father's line item veto. The vulgar commoners think that a line item veto is only reserved for a public politician because the fatherless and vulgar commoners "have no understanding, and only repeat what their rulers are pleased to tell them. To get a referendum accepted or rejected it is only necessary to have it praised or ridiculed in a popular play. ... The upshot of such a democracy is tyranny". - Plato.

In order to understand nature, nature must be understood before there were public governments, when before there were public governments there was only religion and barter, and before there was religion there was only family traditions and barter, therefore, respect must be granted in the following order: families, traditions, religions, and governments coexisting with private and public separations. When a public government evolves into fatherless goons and then dishonors fathers, then that public government will become a failed regime, like the failed regimes of the Athenians and the Romans when their pretentious, pompous, and presumptuous intimidations disregarded families, traditions, and religions then caused a revolt.

It takes a lot of effort to take on a fatherless City of goons that are not willing to accept responsibility for their mistakes. I had to study cultures and laws for several years when there are not many that file in the U.S. Supreme Court, and if the opposition had any issues with that filing they would have filed a response, of which they waived their right to file a response. What I do not want is another living through the mistakes of vulgar commoners from mob-rule and tyranny of the majority that wastes virtue, merit, and time.

ADDRESSING THE U.S. SUPREME COURT

I begin these oral arguments as James Madison began his oral arguments when addressing the House of Representatives regarding amending the Constitution with the Bill of Rights that along with the Fourteenth Amendment are supported in my writ of certiorari. The people "think we are not sincere in our desire to incorporate such amendments in the Constitution as will secure those rights, which they consider as not sufficiently guarded. ... I wish, among other reasons why something should be done, that those who have been friendly to the adoption of this constitution, may have the opportunity of proving to those who were opposed to it, that they were as sincerely devoted to liberty and a republican government, as those who charged them with wishing the adoption of this constitution in order to lay the foundation of an aristocracy or despotism. ... I know some respectable characters who opposed this government on these grounds; but I believe that the great mass of the people who opposed it, disliked it because it did not contain effectual provisions against encroachments on particular rights. ... I think we should obtain the confidence of our fellow citizens, in proportion as we fortify the rights of the people against the encroachments of the government." While James Madison was trying to secure the States against despotism from the newly formed Democracy, what he did not realize was that the people needed security against encroachments of a State when after some States abused their particular power with despotism through the Tenth Amendment, the Constitution was further amended with the Fourteenth Amendment that effectually overrules any despotism from the Tenth Amendment. Then when many States replicated a similar system of Democracy as the Federal Government, then whether Federal or State, James Madison was correct in his apprehension that Democracy could lead to despotism from tyranny of the majority. For example, prior to World War II popular public opinion from the American and German Democracies was trending with a theory from "leading scientists, politicians, and celebrities around the world. Research was funded by distinguished philanthropies, and carried out at prestigious universities. The crisis is reported frequently in the media. The science is taught in college and high school classrooms. Its supporters included Theodore Roosevelt, Woodrow Wilson, and Winston Churchill. It was approved by Supreme Court justices Oliver Wendell Holmes and Louis Brandeis, who ruled in its favor. The famous names who supported it included Alexander Graham Bell, inventor of the telephone; activist Margaret Sanger; botanist Luther Burbank; Leland Stanford, founder of Stanford University; the novelist H.G. Wells; the playwright George Bernard Shaw; and hundreds of others. Nobel Prize winners gave support. Research was backed by the Carnegie and Rockefeller Foundations. The Cold Springs Harbor Institute was built to carry out this research, but important work was also done at Harvard, Yale, Princeton, Stanford, and Johns Hopkins. Legislation to address the crisis was passed in states from New York to California. These efforts had the support of the National Academy of Sciences, the American Medical Association, and the National Research Council. It was said that if Jesus were alive, he would have supported this effort. All in all, the research, legislation, and molding of public opinion surrounding the theory went on for almost a half a century. ... Today, we know that this famous theory that gained so much support was actually pseudoscience. The crisis it claimed was nonexistent. And the actions taken in the name of this theory were morally and criminally wrong. Ultimately, they led to the deaths of millions of people. The theory was eugenics, and its history is so dreadful - and, to those who were caught up in it, so embarrassing - that it is now rarely discussed. But it is a story that should be well known to every citizen, so that its horrors are not repeated. The theory of eugenics postulated a crisis of the gene pool leading to the deterioration of the human race. The best human beings were not breeding as rapidly as the inferior ones" while at that time the inferior ones were stated to be "foreigners, immigrants, Jews, degenerates, the unfit, and the 'feeble minded'. "Francis Galton", a respected British scientist, first speculated about this area, but his ideas were taken far beyond anything he intended. They were adopted by science-minded Americans, as well as those who had no interest in science but who were worried about the immigration of inferior races early in the twentieth century - 'dangerous human pests' who represented 'the rising tide of imbeciles' and who were polluting the best of the human race. The eugenicists and [those opposed to immigration] joined forces to put a stop to this. The plan was to identify individuals who were feeble-minded - [at that time it was stated that] Jews were agreed to be largely feeble-minded, but so were many foreigners, as well as blacks - then stop them from breeding by isolation in institutions or by sterilization. As Margaret Sanger said, 'Fostering the good-for-nothing at the expense of the good is an extreme cruelty ... there is no greater curse to posterity than that of bequeathing them an increasing population of imbeciles' She spoke of the burden of caring for 'this dead weight of human waste'. Such views were widely shared. H.G. Wells spoke against 'ill-trained swarms of inferior citizens'. Theodore Roosevelt said that "Society has no business to permit degenerates to reproduce their kind". Luther Burbank stated: 'Stop permitting criminals and weaklings to reproduce'. George Bernard Shaw said that only eugenics could save mankind. There was overt racism in this movement, exemplified by texts such as 'The Rising Tide of Color against White World Supremacy', by American author Lothrop Stoddard. But, at the time, racism was considered an unremarkable aspect of the effort to attain a marvelous goal - the improvement of humankind in the future. It was this avant-garde notion that attracted the most liberal and progressive minds of a generation. California was one of the twenty-nine American states to pass laws allowing sterilization, but it proved the most forward-looking and enthusiastic - more sterilizations were carried out in California than anywhere in America. Eugenics research was funded by the Rockefeller Foundation. The latter was so enthusiastic that even after the center of the eugenics effort moved to Germany, and involved the gassing of individuals from mental institutions, the Rockefeller Foundation continued to finance German researchers at a very high level. (The foundation was quit about it, but they were still funding research in 1939, only months before the onset of World War II.) Since the 1920's, American eugenicists had been jealous because the Germans had taken leadership of the movement away from them [and] ... set up ordinary-looking houses where 'mental defectives' were brought and interviewed one at a

time, before being led into a back room, which was, in fact,

a gas chamber. There, they were gassed with carbon

monoxide, and their bodies disposed of in a crematorium

located on the property. Eventually, this program was

expanded into a vast network of concentration camps

located near railroad lines, enabling the efficient transport

and killing of ten million undesirables. After World War II,

nobody was a eugenicist, and nobody had ever been a

eugenicist. Biographers of the celebrated and the powerful

did not dwell on the attractions of this philosophy to their

subjects, and sometimes did not mention it at all. Eugenics

ceased to be a subject for college classrooms, although

some argue that its ideas continue to have currency in

disguised form. But in retrospect, three points stand out.

First, despite the construction of Cold Springs Harbor

Laboratory, despite the efforts at universities and the

pleadings of lawyers, there was no scientific basis for

eugenics. In fact, nobody at that time knew what a gene really was. The movement was able to proceed because it employed vague terms never rigorously defined. 'Feeble-mindedness' could mean anything from poverty and illiteracy to epilepsy. Similarly, there was no clear definition of 'degenerate' or 'unfit'. Second, the eugenics movement was really a social program masquerading as a scientific one. What drove it was concern about immigration, and racism and undesirable people moving into one's neighborhood or country. Once again, vague terminology helped conceal what was really going on. Third, and most distressing, the scientific establishment in both the United States and Germany did not mount any sustained protest." - Michael Crichton from Appendix I in his 2004 book: "State of Fear". The aftermath of Court filings from both parties began in July 2004 after I mailed a postcard to my youngest daughter that pictured a rainbow and a smile that others thought a father should not send his daughter, followed by conjecture, harsh inquisition, and despair from

a victimless and tumultuous pillow fight from the totalitarian

socialists of mob-rule with antagonism that think raising

children should be from only one type of factory line or pod

- when what they thought was their factory line or pod

neglected excessive modern divorces and a five million

women surplus with tolerance thereof - then faithlessly and

harshly questioned, coerced and antagonized my daughter

into hatred and slander then forcefully took my sons with

conjecture, slander, and hearsay. Like I wrote in the

Informal Brief: "when what the plaintiff said and what the

plaintiff did was mostly in response to what the plaintiff's

daughter said or did in order to maintain domestic

tranquility and her scholastic achievements", when the

closeness was usually after someone outside the home

depressed my daughter while at the same time I was

maintaining domestic tranquility and scholastic

achievements for my sons. A decade ago some wanted me

to use the word 'ethos', however, I did not want to use a word in the writ of certiorari that a justice might misinterpret since the word ethos contains 'or', therefore the word 'ethos' has been reserved for oral arguments. The moral nature must accompany the distinguishing character, sentiments, and guiding beliefs of a person, group, or institution, therefore, the encroachers, debauchers, adulterers, and slanderers - especially under oath that disregards the guiding beliefs of an institution and community of interests - cannot use the word ethos, especially when they do not have a distinguishing character and sincere sentiments directly involved, therefore, the unscrupulous opposition that encroached cannot apply for the word ethos nor refute my usage of the word ethos. The most disturbing aspect of encroachments is that mob-rule disregards the merit that was achieved and then tries to execute another whether physically or metaphysically when literally or figuratively dismissing the real justice of the peace that secures unalienable rights such as the right of privacy that prevents the belatedly inexperienced from conjecturing and then speculating about what they did not experience. The amicably respectful, amiably tactful, and affably polite forms the best way while respectfully asking her father for her hand in marriage with merit and sincere sentiments rather than physically fighting on the inner-city streets, or mentally fighting with physical inferences in an adversarial Court system of negligence and injustice. The difference between a father and vulgar commoners of mob-rule is that a father tells his daughter to cover up while mob-rule advocates stripping her down while in denial of their degenerative perversions when the result of others insensitively and inappropriately asking her intimate questions was her later stripping down with lewd pictures of herself on the internet, of which a respectable man would not marry such a woman. The vulgar commoners of mob-rule think that a line item veto is only reserved for a public politician rather than a father because the fatherless and vulgar commoners of mob-rule "have no understanding, and only repeat what their rulers are pleased to tell them. To get a referendum accepted or rejected it is only necessary to have it praised or ridiculed in a popular play. ... The upshot of such a democracy is tyranny". - Plato. For example, I reviewed a video released on December 19, 2016 from a 2014 case in the Oklahoma Supreme Court where a woman violently pushed then slapped a man, and then he punched her as if to say do not put your hands on me again bitch. There were two offensive physical assaults from a woman and then a physical response from a man in self-defense. The results were that the pussy whipped men from popular public opinion led by a female public politician stated that he should be kicked off the football team then advocated the alleged victim's lawsuit is acceptable. On one hand the sons of a bitch want gender equality and then on the other hand they discriminate against self-defense

when their foregoing misunderstanding of gender equality

is why I reject popular public opinion from "unscrupulous

flatterers" - Plato. If I was the justice in that case and

reviewed that video the legal action against that man would

be dismissed. The results were that the man whom

physically responded in self-defense after two violent

assaults against him was punished, therefore, the

Oklahoma Court and public media are gender biased when

advocating that a woman can walk up to a man and then

violently assault him multiple times and get away with her

crime while in denial of reality when the foregoing is one of

the reason why there are less modern marriages than in

the past since there are not many men that want to be

assaulted, abused, and enslaved by a woman using a

Government of goons. Popular public opinion must think

like a father after undisciplined children violently attack one

another when either do not get their way or do not like what the other stated. When I grew up it was who hit who first regardless of boy or girl, and that is how I parented while the foregoing justice is inculcated in childhood when growing up in sired gender balances, therefore, justice is not mostly learned from outward education, justice is mostly learned from childhood inculcation. For example, after I had previously went places with my daughter without my sons, and then she discovered I was going four wheeling in the mountains with my sons while requesting that she clean the house, she slapped me in the face. I rationalized with her rather than physically retaliate, however, if she pushed and then slapped me, I would not rule out an immediate physical response when a father should not spare the rod and spoil the child without discipline and work ethic that involves chores when not many men want to marry a woman whom refuses to clean the house, and is one of the reasons why their mother lost custody after a judge told her it does not matter how much money you have there is no excuse for not cleaning the house.

The Department of Social Services neglected a sired gender balance and merited functional family that dismisses a backstabbing prostitute that faithlessly advocates a belatedly wretched, miserable, and treacherous betrayal from a regression into their fatherless mother's wretched, miserable, and treacherous betrayals using unscrupulous flatterers of popular public opinion.

In order to understand nature, nature must be understood before there were public governments, when before there were public governments there was only religion and barter, and before there was religion there was only family traditions and barter, therefore, respect must be granted in the following order: families, traditions, religions, and governments peacefully coexisting with private and public separations. When a public government evolves into fatherless goons and dishonors fathers, then that public government will become a failed regime, like the failed regimes of the Athenians and Romans when their pretentious, pompous, and presumptuous intimidations disregarded families, traditions, and religions then caused a revolt. It takes much effort to take on a fatherless City of faithless goons that are not willing to accept responsibility for their mistaken encroachments and entanglements. At the moment it appears that Senior and Junior made it to the United States Supreme Court with justices in the middle, although, the junior representing the former Director of Social Services can be considered as a spurious imposter and a fraud rather than my son. Third party involvement began before the year 2000 when the landlord that rented out to the mother of my youngest three children called and told me about the deteriorated conditions that my children were living in. I had already been building something better for my children since I already knew that their mother was incapable while the popular public belated flatterers had degenerately thought I was building something better for only a couple. In the year 2000, after I gained judicial custody of my children, and two weeks before I gained physical custody, their mother tried to seduce me, of which I rejected, after I was remarried and mostly concerned about improving my sired children. In 2004 their mother again deteriorated conditions while seducing unscrupulous flatterers from popular public opinion who ironically stated my relationship with my daughter had something to do with their mother when I wanted something better than their fatherless mother when what was better was from traditionally inherited, directed, and patterned from their father in due respect of the safety and well-being for every sired child. The more that others defer to popular public opinion the more they become degenerated from unscrupulous flatterers. For example,

Hollywood made showing cleavage with fake breast

implants popular and publically accepted after it was a

taboo 40 years ago. It is distracting how Hollywood only

wants to accept a taboo if that taboo does not oppose

their salacious profiteering. I am not deferring to

unscrupulous flatterers with social programs from

salacious profiteers. Paraphrasing from Michael

Crichton's book, so that its horrors are not repeated, do

not defer to social programs from totalitarian

socialists with votes from vulgar commoners of mob-

rule using pseudoscience rather than real science. After

encroachments, the intruders eventually discovered

poetic forms and artistic drawings of life, liberty, and

happiness from a sired gender balance and merited

functional family. I do not want another father and civil

citizen living through the extraneous interferences,

excessive entanglements, and tumultuous

encroachments from tyranny of the majority in denial of

their degenerative perversions that waste potency, virtue,
merit, and time when invading privacy, faithlessly
conjecturing, plundering sired children, potsherd
gambling, ostracizing, charging, incarcerating, forcing
harmful drugs, and stealing intellectual properties while
depriving substantive due process and politically playing
gladiator games to dramatically entertain and profiteer
with vulgar commoners, totalitarian socialists,
unscrupulous flatterers, and crowds of intruders.

CONCLUSION

Justice is not encroaching and coercing another to
act a common way while harmfully depriving liberty,
justice is respecting the property and rights that secures
liberty without substantially harming another; therefore,
a civil citizen can conclude that this petitioner deserves
due recompense.

DISSENT

On January 17th, 2017 the writ of certiorari was denied without reason nor provision for oral arguments. While I made a sincere effort to support every race in my Court filings, the facts are that the worse years of my life were on Barrack Obama's watch. A few days after his inauguration I was incarcerated and a few days before he left office the United States Supreme Court writ was denied. I believe the foregoing is more than a coincidence since one of my Court filings revealed Obama's advocacy for strip mining in his published book, and since Federal judges are appointed by the executive branch they had a conflict of interest while another reason could be that the U.S. Supreme Court judges were negligent and/or inferior and did not want a challenge because while it is easy for them to intimidate lawyers that risk their license and future earnings, a pro se plaintiff has minimal risk and can tell them like it is.

The word dissent is ambiguous after the real majority must always be from biological fathers when what happens if vulgar commoners of mob-rule vote from popular public opinion and form a pseudo majority? The result can be a dissent that can be applied to either party while that dissent has been debated throughout history using similar words with different definitions such as religion or religious, or secular or religious while in history those definitions have been separated with private property that oppose encroachments.

When I grew up, if you went in the rural parts of the Country you would see "No Trespassing" signs posted on private property that usually included the word "risk", meaning if you thought you could use that private property for common use, you could get shot, or you might get lucky and the owner would give only a warning shot, or call the Sheriff and the trespasser would get a verbal warning or paper ticket to show up for Court like when I filed an Amended Complaint and the Sheriff served the defendants. When many in the cities have never been out of the cities and think they can vote to trespass and use another's private property as common property with their sleazy vulgar gangs, they risk their life. The foregoing is the U.S. Second Amendment that I recall when growing up. Other than losing manufacturing jobs, disrespecting religion and the U.S. Second Amendment are reasons why the sleazy vulgar Democrats lost the last election.

During Social Service visitations with my sons, and after my sons visited their mother unsupervised, and then visited their father in a supervised visitation, junior ran out of the visitation and opened up the hoods of multiple vehicles owned by other people. What if an owner of one of those vehicles observed a juvenile delinquent opening the hood of their vehicle?

No respect for another's property is what you get from sleazy vulgar fatherless gangs while encroachments by others on my private property prove that they were raised by sleazy vulgar trash. What if I tell junior that his punishment for emotionally choosing his mother over his father that raised better is that his father's declaration is that junior recklessly disregarded the wretched and miserable defects on his mother's side that led to epilepsy when what if I eugenically dismiss his mother's side as genetically defective? What if I tell him that his mother ironically stated his father was from a bad seed while neglecting his father's sired gender balance and merited functional family while his fatherless mother was only from the popular Cinderella theory that later imploded when absent of merit? What if he ungratefully dishonored his father, and then his father destroyed that son of bitch?

The reason for forgiving is because psychoanalytically a son needs to spend more time with his father no later than six years old, however, junior was two years late and had a difficult time detaching from his mother, therefore, my junior is more dysfunctional than most sons. The Greek educated were more curious about a female Electra complex while neglecting a male Oedipus complex where if either complex is abruptly detached with extraneous interferences then that can cause ungratefulness, homosexuality, and/or borderline personality disorder, therefore, the best way is when father and mother set aside differences, and in the best interest of their child pass their child back and forth until their child's complex has been peacefully resolved.

Social Services states they know what is in the best interest of the child, although, Social Services does not know what is in the best interest of the child because they have proven to be interested in only accessorizing the mother with theft while ignorantly thinking giving money and material items without merit will solve the children's deficiencies, inadequacies, and inferiorities.

The vulgar commoners, totalitarian socialists, and unscrupulous flatterers cannot be trusted when they have advocated extraneous interferences, excessive entanglements, and tumultuous encroachments.

Most of the contentious quarreling from a dissent can be dismissed when respectfully asking her father for her hand in marriage while respecting merit and sincere sentiments rather than coercively taking her using a socialistic totalitarian Government of goons that wretchedly and miserably flunked. Those that encroached think they got away with their libelous slander after dismissing my legitimate claim when now the public needs to know there is no civil U.S. justice system that they can depend on and that changes need to be made to public policy, therefore, my last protest is writing this book for ISBN publication for addressing

International Human Rights that prevents a public

Government from "interfering with his privacy, family,

home or correspondence, nor attacks upon his honor

and reputation". If I knew in July 2004 the U.S. Justice

system could be an accomplice to coercing against

their father whom taught his children merit and sincere

sentiments and then others debauched healthy, happy,

and successful children that did not substantially harm

another while encroaching and incarcerating their father

for multiple years while forcing harmful drugs and

depriving substantive due process, I would have

exercised the United States Second Amendment in July

2004. I understand why there are more killings in U.S.

cities than most Countries since why trust the

negligence and injustice of the totalitarian socialists that

without merit nor real considerations make sleazy

excuses to encroach, subjugate, and coercively plunder

a man's earnings, his woman, his children, and his property, when if that becomes popular then many dissenters will stockpile weapons like when "Protests in the rural Massachusetts turned into direct action in August 1786, after the state legislature adjourned without considering the many petitions that had been sent to Boston. On August 29 a well-organized force of protestors, Shays among them, marched on Northampton and successfully prevented the county court from sitting. The leaders of this and later forces proclaimed that they were seeking relief from the burdensome judicial processes that were depriving the people of their land and possessions." - Wikipedia, "Daniel Shays", "Protests against the courts". "Shay's Rebellion was an armed uprising in Massachusetts ... during 1786 and 1787. Revolutionary War veteran Daniel Shays led four thousand rebels ... in an uprising against perceived economic and civil rights injustices". -

Wikipedia, "Shays' Rebellion". The foregoing is the real reason for the executive branch and Bill of Rights, then when others deprived citizens an equal right for property and liberty is the real reason for the Fourteenth Amendment, therefore, I filed an Amended Complaint after the State encroached on my private property then attempted to claim my private property was their public property while depriving liberty and then attempting to enslave me in my own home when if this single man army had attached explosives to Social Services others would have told a different story about why I thought about the foregoing. If I was President of the United States my executive order and U.S. Supreme Court nominees would be for restricting the power of the State while any ordered child support would only cover the necessities. I believe the foregoing secures civil rights and puts more value on amicable trade and raising merited children for a better economy in the future.

Amendment I

The Director of Social Services can be compared to Richard Nixon that discriminated and encroached then plundered confidential intellectual properties from another party that supports a sired gender balance and merited functional family.

The way peace works is respectfully asking her father for her hand in marriage, for example, my eldest daughter's first long term boyfriend asked me for my eldest daughter's hand in marriage. He was a friendly guy and I spent a weekend camping with him and my eldest daughter on an island in the middle of Lake Norman, North Carolina, and we had fun. The only issue with my daughter's boyfriend was he had an unstable childhood, was on mental medication, and my eldest daughter had just joined the Air Force. He had sincere feelings for my eldest daughter and from empathy this was one of the most difficult decisions I ever made in my life. In the best interest of my eldest daughter I had to say no. The next two men did not ask me for my eldest daughter's hand in marriage and they ended in divorce. Before my eldest daughter married the next man I told him he should marry her, then in early 2017 my eldest daughter told family members that this is the happiest she has been in her life. As for my youngest daughter, I did everything I could to protect her. The mistake she made is after those that were jealous started questioning her harshly she should have said talk to my father or ask my father rather than trying to answer questions herself and then after repressed she started slandering of which led others to slander.

He loves her and she loves popularity. Prosecutors argued in June 2017 that Michelle Carter "used his suicide to get from friends the attention that she desperately craved." Many men would rather love a woman regardless of popularity, and if he deeply loves her and then she betrays, then the results are unpredictable, from suicide, regardless of gender, or killing another. When most men are in the presence of a woman being provocative then that becomes popular among men, and if she craves that attention she might cheat on her boyfriend or husband while the man she cheats with could be cheating on his girlfriend or wife when either can cause unpredictable consequences. What is not popular in America is a woman covering herself like in some sects of the Muslim religion while at the same time the intent on reducing the lust in public is safer and more peaceful. The commoners would rather criticize or kill those that cover their women because they are vulgar and would rather look at another's body or talk about another's body rather than get to know and love a woman before any lust is considered. Religiously the Ten Commandments have safety considerations built in countering vulgarity of popularity.

On June 14th 2017, a socialist shot at Republicans. What is a socialist? A socialist evolves from welfare-state policies after "Democracy comes into being" while the gangs form a socialistic party of Nazi's that lead to the Socialistic Nationalist Party "after the poor conquered their opponents" and then form the Gestapo that carry out genocide while "slaughtering some and banishing the rest". The socialistic welfare-state wants free health care and free upper education while in denial of supporting unstable and unmerited childhoods, rather than the working class of Republicans that support merited families and stable childhoods that build wealth and distribute thereof in religions and charities.

I was raising a prudently perfect and merited family that considered prepubescent children and on the last day that we were together I hugged my children while my youngest son was prepubescent and could somewhat however not completely understand the closeness in the family, and then in the aftermath I grieved after others corrupted my youngest son.

In the initial aftermath their mother was worried about what I was going to tell my sons. First, nothing needed to be said to others about a personal and private father and daughter relationship until their mother sleazily gossiped with others about a father and daughter relationship. Second, if my daughter decided to live with her mother then at that time I would have said to my sons that "your mother recklessly disregarded your sister's education and then your sister ran off with some boy. When you meet a girl make sure that you are on good terms with her father". Nothing else needed to be said while father and sons would have continued the amicable relationships while at least one of my sons would have graduated from College if not for the vulgarity of popularity that disrupted their bright future.

Religiously the case is not complicated when my daughter remained a virgin while her relationships while she was a virgin should have remained personal and private, and then whomever took her virginity, or conspired with others to take her virginity, can become public knowledge and is why I write about the irony of the debauchers and those in denial of conspiring to debauch.

In June 2017 I was at Union Station in Washington D.C. and noticed a mother looking over her shoulder at her prepubescent children that she gave cell phones to because the children pressured her into doing the same as popular public opinion while I could tell that their mother was worrying about what those children were doing on their cell phones. If I was their father I would have demanded their mother not listen to popularity and waited until the children were adolescent before exposing them to the vulgarity of popularity.

How about the City representatives strip mined and only listened to slander and then stereotyped and were sent to hell while influencing Eve to listen to the evil branch of tabloids and was condemned to hell? What if after an absolute sired gender balance and merited functional family from a scientific calculation resulted in improving Adam and Eve? I prefer freedom rather than have my every movement scrutinized by the public paparazzi and the unscrupulous tabloids. How about after other sired gender balances and merited functional families discovered the same, and then wanted me to resolve the conflicts on our behalf? What if we did not have enough votes as the votes collected by the slanderous devil? Should we secure private property or go to war?

After researching history and visiting Cities and noting street names and landmarks that were populated prior to 1776, I believe the King of England thought of

America as his pet project for the Queen of England that influenced Cities such as Charlotte N.C. The only issue the King was worried about was collecting taxes for the resources that he distributed in building and protecting many of those Cities. When the people living in America rejected what they believed were excessive taxes and rebelled, the King sent in what could be referred to as the Queen's Marines. The rebels referred to their rebellion as the opposition to tyranny and dissolved political bands while fighting the Queen's Marines and then blamed everything on the King.

What happens after centuries later when America creates a branch of the Military known as the Marines and trains in that it is their responsibility to protect their mother and Country? What if America again becomes the pet project for some Queen with tyranny of the majority and the Marines attack? What if after the U.S. Constitution, Thomas Jefferson and James Madison worried about tyranny of the majority and granted citizens' rights? What if those rights are recklessly disregarded? What we should do is again dissolve political bands and dismantle what Eisenhower cautiously warned as the Military Industrial Complex.

I work with several professionals whom were born in other Countries and they are as peaceful, or more peaceful, than American born people. There is now a President of the United States that is mostly friendly with other Countries while the only time he is dismissive of people in other Countries are the people with ideologies associated with the attack on September 11th 2001, or Countries that have trade imbalances. The legislative branch and some news organizations now want to take back executive power to continue their war mongering. They think they can step into the affairs of another Country and create sanctions on whomever they want. What makes 5 % of the world's population think they are better than 95 % of the world's population? It is the extraneous and offensive rhetoric that causes wars. If they think Democracy is the better Government then what if the world was a Democracy? Then 5 % of the world's population, such as the WWII German Democracy, would not rule the world. Why is it that most families and State Governments condemn violence while National Governments cause violence? There are some National Governments that are like families and give little consideration to creating a military. I believe that it is hypocritical to on one hand condemn violence and on the other hand condone violence. Just because there are borders, of which I believe is more for economic purposes, does not mean that people can become violent. It is only when the barbarous encroach and attack is when there is a need to counter attack in defense. When considering economic borders, the thought of a Global economy is absurd and only serves corporate boards and business owners that move jobs to other Countries. It is a domino effect whereas when some businesses start to move jobs overseas for less expensive labor then many businesses move jobs overseas for competitive reasons when it is the Government's responsibility to enforce tariffs to prevent businesses from neglecting fellow citizens. Regarding minimum wage increases to keep up with a competitive rental market, inevitably excessive minimum wage increases will cause inflation on other necessities. Perhaps there is a compromise between Capitalism and Communism, whereas necessities should be non-profit organizations and non-necessities could be free market Capitalism. The intrusive political vacillations only wastes time with their belated suspense and drama to entertain voters when I could have accomplished more during the same time if the intruders did not slow me down and waste my time.

Others wasting my time caused a continual tax increase when centuries ago Americans fought for no taxes and then centuries later there are more taxes than ever before while the fallacy of Hollywood ironically turns away more than they support. There was a time when the strictest code from religion only expected a flat rate of 10 percent taxes from everyone and then after centuries of dysfunction many are paying more taxes than ever before to support the vulgar commoners advertised by Hollywood that profligates rather than building and establishing a real foundation that can support the future. With all of the dysfunction surrounding us it is impossible for the Republicans to rewind to a time where a flat rate of 10 percent can support everyone. The best tact is supporting biological fathers and real working families while the more the foregoing is supported the more we can incrementally prosper and reduce taxes.

At minimum, ten years ago I could have applied for the same job that I have now and been hired as a professional, and peaceful protester. What happened during the last ten years? Who are the perpetrators that wasted the last ten years? The perpetrators are swindlers and thieves in denial of encroaching, betraying and ripping off a legitimate father. Whom specifically are the perpetrators? Their mother's illegitimate boyfriend, the Iredell County Department of Social Services, the State of N.C., and what was discovered as the illegitimate U.S. Government.

If the aforementioned debauchers knew what true love was they would not be asking what would have happened when there is no unilateral force regarding true love when true love can only happen when two people feel the same way and make statements such as "we feel the same way" as was stated. I do not recall forcing a unilateral decision regarding closeness, there was always a consensual choice while either mostly came and went as they pleased, and that is why I stated neither can state what would have happened when always considering how one another felt in person.

From my prior experience I already knew that women are untrustworthy, therefore, I knew that I had to save every artistic expression. While there was more poetic art expressed than most relationships, I saved virginity while others took virginity without considering any artistic forms, therefore, there is more irony.

Since neither my eldest daughter's mother and I, nor my youngest daughter's mother and I, were still together, neither of my daughters had any real experience about how a man whom dated her should treat her, therefore, before I was about to let my eldest daughter date I took her out and treated her how I expected a man to treat her. At that time my eldest daughter was grateful and then I let her date others only to find out that she later went to a party with some drunken High Schoolers, got drunk and lost her virginity, and then wanted to get away from that boy and moved to her mother's place, of which formed a precedent for a better way in treating my youngest daughter while the Myrtle Beach S.C. vacation was supposed to be the end of the linear example, however, my youngest daughter refused to leave my room after I had already decided she could date others after returning from her mother's visitation. What was frustrating is I had treated her better than any other woman in my life and then she did the most damage when only considering popular public ignorant voting that does not consider sired gender balances and merited functional families nor census gender counts.

Their mother was a bar tender that catered to the inner-city sleuths until she found a barbarous man that sired only girls without any sired sons. What would a lesbian extinction be like if a girl could not find a sired son from a potent and real man?

In June 2017 the U.S. Supreme Court rejected an Arkansas law that prohibited a lesbian spouse of the birth mother from being listed on the birth certificate. Even if I was to abstain in the voting on same sex marriages favored by the 2015 U.S. Supreme Court, how can anyone legitimately and rightfully vote no against the foregoing Arkansas law?

The dysfunctional public only wants to believe a woman when they are the weakest link, and when they are under harsh pressure they start slandering. It was only after slander that I commanded control and that is the only time I starting making unilateral decisions because those that slander have no credibility.

The reason their mother has no credibility is because after the custody hearing I called her and asked what about the slander and she said "so what, I won" and then handed the phone to her boyfriend. The win at all costs mentality, regardless of cheating, is if the U.S. Justice System lets the cheaters get away with their malicious intent, then not only does the U.S. Justice System flunk, their negligence brings the U.S. Second Amendment into consideration.

I have uttered the word bitch every few days for the last 13 years, and sometimes I would find myself uttering the word bitch multiple times a day and would have to think about something else to prevent me from becoming a continuously negative person like most people that work in law enforcement.

I recall a story in South Carolina about a woman whom met another man and then strapped her prior husband's children into the back seat of an SUV and then rolled the SUV into a lake and then her prior husband's children drowned to death.

What I find offensive is that North Carolina ironically stated rape while I saved virginity, and then the State told their mother to take my youngest daughter to the doctor for a legalized debauching. I do not give a damn what type of piece of paper they have on their wall from the University of WWII Germany, they are lucky that I did not immediately kill the belated intruders that only want to stereotype and stigmatize when relying on impotent opinions while I mostly ignored that Government of goons after they think what happened against my eldest daughter at that drunken High Schooler party with their unproven Big Bang theory is more appropriate while thinking slander is more acceptable.

Just like when my youngest daughter came home from her mother's sick and then after I cared for her for a couple of days, and then drove her to the doctor's office, and then after he approached her the first question he asked her was how she felt about her father, and then when the immediate and unequivocal response was in my favor his instinct was to back off and then tell me what he advised I give my daughter while I thought that some of his prescription was a little too touchy and feely at that time. The way nature works is either men respect her father or risk their life while I can reference many songs that state the same.

My decision making process is as pure as any other while the opposition was not present during real time decisions then belatedly conjecture, speculate, stereotype and stigmatize after impotent, inexperienced and popular public belated opinions that are void of sincere sentiments and not worthy of consideration.

I read a U.S. Supreme Court writing that stated puritans versus cavaliers while after experiencing the foregoing then studying a Greek philosopher whom was against the first Athenian Democracy and mentioned the unscrupulous flatterers, then the unscrupulous flatterers can be considered as cavaliers, therefore, the unscrupulous flatterers are the unscrupulous cavaliers.

I believe that the New Testament, similar to the Athenian Democracy, was influenced by popular public opinion. After my father as Jesse and son as David from the Old Testament sired a lineage that the New Testament claims Mary arose from, the New Testament went too far and actually tried to change the traditional lineage from father and son to a woman after many men died in wars while the widows with his children were proselytized from the New Testament and then that culture was preached and then popularly accepted. The New Testament attempts to uphold an unscientific conception and step-father with a spurious imposter named Jesus using his imagination and then trying to preach without knowing his biological and real father. The Old Testament does not believe in the image of an idol while the New Testament made Jesus an idol. The Old Testament believes in proportional trade while the New Testament believes in disproportionate trade. The Old Testament does not believe in coveting thy neighbor while the New Testament believes in forgiving the trespasses on thy neighbor. The Old Testament believes in eye for an eye while the New Testament does not believe in self-defense. The Old Testament has laws against prostitution while Jesus washes the feet of a prostitute. I state that we should stop giving away sired sons to be killed in wars and then we will limit the politicians, prostitutes, widows, and unrelated preachers while saving sired sons.

If another has a philosophy of stopping war then what we can agree on is stopping war while the answer is not a gap. The best answer is stop the vulgar commoners from encroaching while respecting and asking her father for her hand in marriage, and if her father says no, then debate him genuinely from sincere sentiments and a plan for future support without bringing in the popular public politicians, prostitutes, swindlers, gamblers, and salacious profiteers that wastes the time of everyone.

The answer is we improve and perfect rather than rifle through a time before improvements and then try to criticize one another. What I like most about professionals in the private sector is that most professionals consider suggestions for improvement rather than the public sector of personal attacks from the poor that advocate popular public political profiteering and more taxes. The issue with the unrestrained and underdeveloped is they have children they cannot support while relying on excessive taxation.

The way a peaceful family works is that a father and mother work together in harmony without stating anything negative against one another in front of their children even if they have differences and argue with one another in private. When my sons were in my custody I never directly stated anything negative about their mother in front of them while I expected their mother not to say anything negative about their father in front of the children. If she had a disagreement about how I treated my children then she should have talked to me in private rather than bring in another man and what Reagan cautiously warned as the welfare-state to swindle and plunder.

Most people are respectful and grateful for their father, regardless of how much time spent with them because if not for their father they would not exist. Most of the opposition are from people whom did not know there father and only try to make sleazy excuses for what they did not experience so they can think they are more like others when they are not when not knowing their father and then trying to disrespect their father.

Now let us consider what the general consensus of many Department of Social Services consider and that is should parents spank their children. Social Services states no while let us consider the only time I spanked my youngest daughter as a lesson. Less than a year after I was awarded custody and before I refined my youngest daughter, the public school system called me and told me that she violently threw a book at another student. Is a mental timeout, as Social Services suggests, an eye for an eye or even an equal measure, or should she physically feel some pain so that she can experience what that other student felt when she violently hit the other student with a book? I chose spanking her, and then she never became violent with another student, therefore, I made the correct decision while Social Services only tries to dictate what can at times be an ineffective waste of time. How many social psychologists with Degrees participated in the genocide of WWII? Did they forget that their Democratic and typical majority was defeated by Americans respecting private property separations?

It is convenient for the fatherless and debauchers to think there is no authority from biological fathers when trying to enslave and plunder his earnings while trying to stereotype, stigmatize and control families, take sired sons under the New Testament and military industrial complex, then debauch sired daughters while continuing their degenerations with more Democratic ignorance that raises minimum wage without restraining business trade while businesses continue to send jobs to other countries to find lower wages while the currency in other countries become stronger and the American dollar becomes weaker, then raising taxes on the working class while unrestrained businesses horde cash overseas to avoid paying corporate taxes.

When considering the strongest beliefs throughout history that formed civilization, the Old Testament can be considered as the Republicans and the New Testament can be considered as Democrats. For example, the Democratic Barrack Obama that advocated strip mining is mostly fatherless and supported only his mother's side at the Democratic Convention while Donald Trump presented testimonials from his sired and merited children at the Republican Convention. Barrack Obama supported Hillary Clinton that won the popular vote while Donald Trump won the more prestigious electoral vote and won the United States election. In the Civil war the Democrats advocated slavery while the Republicans advocated abolishing slavery. The Athenians as Democrats were proselytized by the New Testament and only rely on popular public opinions (votes) without considering merit and gender counts from the Romans as Republicans while father and son, proclaimed as men in the Declaration of Independence and United States Constitution separated from oppression when excluding votes from the Queen and women. Obviously there is some contention, controversy and differences of opinion throughout history while separations prevent encroachments and broadcasting to the premature when only considering popular public votes that lead to "Democracy comes into being, after the poor conquer their opponents, slaughtering some and banishing the rest" while not considering health nor merit nor securing *civil* rights with a code that is "adequate in courtesy or politeness" and "in connection with private rights and obligations", "not military or ecclesiastical".

Unlike the mother in question that had more than 50 police calls to her house before my custody, there were no public disturbances nor police calls at my residence of 333 North Greenbrier Road in Statesville, North Carolina until Democracy encroached and caused disturbances after June 5th 2004.

In every modern public place women stand in line wearing skin tight clothes and showing cleavage, and if that is not enough for the slanderous devil to tempt his fellow man how about what I observed on my way to work where a woman in a miniskirt tempted a man when riding up a three story escalator while daring a man to come on to her so that she can seductively lure him into sexual relations, and then try to charge and break him. I do not agree with women preying on the potency of man and then relying on other men to believe in the seductress and then have those men betray his fellow man.

The aftermath is all about neglecting encroachments and misinterpreting misinformation in front of an ignorant popular public grand jury. After many years of their misinterpretations, they have no victim, therefore I could have developed a vigilante bomb and destroyed their Federal Court building, especially when the Federal Court did not respect my *civil* lawsuit against a police-state that could not bring forth a victim. Perhaps if the Federal Courts neglect my writings then another might not consider the negligent judiciary and then immediately counter attack with substantial harm.

There were about 100 people shot and 14 killed during the July 4th 2017 week in Chicago IL., where Barrack Obama had represented as a Senator. Obama is lucky that his advocacy of strip mining did not result in a vigilante father, whom had not substantially harmed another, attach explosives with more dead after a woman with a Government encroached. ie: Oklahoma City bombing in 1995 responding to Janet Reno and the U.S. Government in 1993 encroaching in Waco Texas.

The 1995 Oklahoma City bombing followed the 1993 siege in Waco Texas and the 1992 siege in Ruby Ridge, Idaho which were the declaration of causes for the Oklahoma City bombing orchestrated by Timothy McVeigh, a U.S. Army Veteran whom was trained by the U.S. Government to uphold the U.S. Constitution and Amendments thereof. McVeigh wore a printed T-shirt with the motto of the Commonwealth of Virginia, "Sic semper tyrannis" meaning "thus always to tyrants", from what Brutus said when he assassinated Caesar. An envelope of his was found with revolutionary materials that included a bumper sticker with the Thomas Jefferson slogan: "When the government fears the people, there is liberty. When the people fear the government, there is tyranny." Underneath, McVeigh wrote, "Maybe now, there will be liberty!" with a hand copied quote by John Locke asserting that a man has a right to kill someone who takes away his liberty.

The 1993 siege in Waco, Texas was after a religious group known as the Branch Davidians had peaceably assembled families and formed a religious community on private property while teaching the moral principles in the Bible. Many of the members of the religious group had been involved with the Davidians for a few generations, and many had large families, and were friendly with the locals. Over the prior years, there were hostilities against the religious group arising from a few disgruntled ex-members, and then after misinformation was disseminated, others used stereotypical stigmatizing allegations. In defense of religious liberty, the Davidians began stockpiling weapons of which attracted the attention of the Alcohol, Tobacco and Firearm Administration. The weapon purchases were legal while one of the religious group members was a federal firearms licensed dealer and operated a retail gun business and traded at gun shows, and while there were some legal weapon parts in stock that could be assembled into illegal weapons, the weapon parts were never assembled by the Davidian members into illegal weapons. After the ATF stated the weapon parts could be assembled into illegal weapons, a search warrant was granted to search for illegal weapons.

"The ATF attempted to execute their search warrant on a Sunday morning, February 28th, 1993. Any advantage of surprise was lost when a KWTX-TV reporter who had been tipped off about the raid, asked for directions from a U.S. Postal Service mail carrier who was coincidently David Koresh's brother-in-law. Koresh then told undercover ATF agent Robert Rodriquez that they knew a raid was imminent. Rodriquez had infiltrated the Branch Davidians and was astonished to find that his cover had been blown. The agent made an excuse and left the compound. When asked later what the Branch Davidians had been doing when he left the compound, Rodriquez replied, 'They were praying.' Branch Davidian survivors have written that Koresh ordered selected male followers to begin arming and taking up defensive positions, while the women and children were told to take cover in their rooms. Koresh told them he would try to speak to the agents, and what happened next would depend on the agents' intentions. Despite being informed that the Branch Davidians knew a raid was coming, the ATF commander ordered that the raid go ahead, even though their plan depended on reaching the compound without the Branch Davidians being armed and prepared. While not standard procedure, ATF agents had their blood type written on their arms or neck after leaving the staging area and before the raid, because it was recommended by the military to facilitate speedy blood transfusions in the case of injury. ATF agents stated that they heard shots coming from within the compound, while Branch Davidian survivors claimed that the first shots came from the ATF agents outside. A suggested reason may have been an accidental discharge of a weapon, possibly by an ATF agent, causing the ATF to respond with fire from automatic weapons. Other reports claim the first shots were fired by the ATF 'dog team' sent to kill the dogs in the Branch Davidian kennel. ... During the first shots, Koresh was wounded, shot in the wrist. Within a minute of the raid, Branch Davidian Wayne Martin called emergency services, pleading for them to stop shooting. The resident asked for a cease fire, and audiotapes record him saying, 'Here they come again!' and, 'That's them shooting! That's not us!'" – Wikipedia.

What followed was exchanging gun fire for two hours with approximately the same number of dead on either side, and then after the ATF was running low on ammunition a cease fire was agreed.

After the cease fire the Branch Davidians allowed the ATF dead and wounded to be evacuated and held their fire during the ATF retreat. After six hours of the cease fire a Branch Davidian, whom was returning from work outside the compound and attempting to enter the compound, was shot once in the eye, once in the heart, and five times in the back.

At first the Davidians had telephone contact with the local news media, and David Koresh gave phone interviews, and then after the FBI became involved, the FBI cut Davidian communication to the outside world, and then the only communication with those inside was by telephone from a group of 25 FBI negotiators. During the days that followed the siege David Koresh released children between the ages of 12 and 19. There were then 98 adults and 23 children remaining inside while David Koresh stated God wanted him to wait inside.

On day nine of the standoff, the Davidians sent out a
video tape to show there were no hostages and that
everyone was staying inside on their own free will.
David Koresh then ordered 11 more people to leave
while negotiating for more time to write religious
documents. After the FBI negotiators' reviewed the
video tape, the FBI thought if they released the tape to
the media then that would gain sympathy for David
Koresh and the Davidians.

In the attempt to force the Davidians out, the FBI tried
using sleep deprivation by using all-night broadcasts of
jet planes, pop music, chanting, and the screams of
rabbits being slaughtered. The FBI used military
vehicles to destroy perimeter fencing, outbuildings, and
crushing cars belonging to the Davidians while
repeatedly driving over the grave of a Davidian founder
despite protests from the Davidians remaining inside.

The FBI eventually cut the power and water to the compound, forcing those inside to survive on rain water and rations. Janet Reno stated the FBI was tired of waiting and that the standoff was costing a million dollars a week. After 51 days of the standoff, the FBI launched tear gas attacks to force the Davidians out, and then after six hours of tear gas attacks, none of the Davidians left the building, and then three fires broke out almost simultaneously in different parts of the building. Only 9 people left the building during the fire. The remaining Davidians, including the children, were either buried alive by rubble, suffocated by smoke or carbon monoxide inhalation, or shot. Koresh's top aide shot and killed Koresh and then killed himself. While the government maintains the fires were started by the Davidians, they do not accept responsibility for the speculation and conjecture to obtain a search warrant to infringe on religious liberty and peaceful assembly.

The difference in my religious practice and the Waco

Texas religious practice is I did not combine the First

and Second Amendment then stockpile weapons to

protect religious liberty, as was the case in Waco

Texas, because I believed the Government would civilly

uphold the First Amendment without needing weapons.

How many poor people that run up to a welfare-state to

get a weapon and a welfare-check to become

barbarous did Obama employ to degenerate and track

my movements? The poor are incapable of appreciating

improvement and then increase taxes to employ a

police-state that charge without a victim while the

Judiciary branch neglects spurious charges and

wrongful incarcerations after "Democracy comes into

being, after the poor conquer their opponents,

slaughtering some and banishing the rest."

In the 1992 case of Ruby Ridge in Idaho, after

reading several reports over the years, I believe what

attracted agents to Randy Weaver, a former Iowa factory worker and U.S. Army combat engineer whom moved to Idaho with his wife Vicki to home school their children to escape what they thought was a corrupted world, were Randy's racial associations against Zionist organizations and posting racial signs on his private property of which while legal, much like posting signs for candidate elections, posting racial signs are not the best tact for a City, Community, State, or Nation. If a person has racial interests, the best tact is discretion. What followed was entrapment from an ATF informant selling a sawed off shot gun cut a ½" under the legal limit to Randy Weaver, then charged Randy Weaver.

After Randy Weaver did not appear at the original Court date, U.S. Marshalls sieged Randy Weaver's private property, first throwing rocks at Randy's cabin to provoke his dog while Kevin, whom is an adult family friend, and Randy's 14 year old son Samuel emerged and followed the dog to investigate. The U.S. Marshalls identified themselves and told Kevin and Samuel to back off of which they did when retreating from the woods to an open area where a U.S. Marshall shot and killed the dog, then Samuel yelled "you shot my dog, you son of a bitch" and then fired back and continued to retreat, and then a U.S. Marshall shot and killed Samuel in the back, then Kevin shot and killed a U.S. Marshall. Randy and Vicki retrieved Samuel's body and placed the body in a cabin near the main cabin. On the next day of the siege, Randy, his teenage daughter Sara, and Kevin went to check on Randy's dead son, and then after opening a shed door, Randy was shot and wounded in the back by an F.B.I. sniper. While Randy, Sara, and Kevin ran back to the cabin, Vicki, while holding their infant baby behind a partially opened door and waiting for Randy, Sara, and Kevin to return, was shot through the door and killed by an F.B.I. sniper.

The total shots on the first day of the siege were 14 submachine gun rounds by U.S. Marshalls against 5 rounds from Samuel's .223 Ruger Mini-14 and Kevin's .30-06 hunting rifle.

"To answer public questions about Ruby Ridge, the Senate Subcommittee on Terrorism, Technology and Government Information held a total of 14 days of hearings between September 6 and October 19, 1995, and subsequently issued a report calling for reforms in federal law enforcement to prevent a repeat of the losses of life at Ruby Ridge." - Wikipedia

After closing on a property a few weeks ago in a suburb of a small City that can be considered as a rural part of the Country, then shopping at Rural King, of which is more like a combination of Tractor Supply and Wal-Mart known to most people in the Country, to pick up a professional chainsaw to fell a dead widow maker on my property, and observing the demographic, the demographic reminded me of reuniting with relatives in Georgia. After returning to the metropolis of Washington D.C. and watching television, I am reminded how most of television is out of touch with the reality of rural living since television mostly caters to the densities in the Cities to maximize profits, much like how Obama was elected when using inner-city street gangs such as the Black Panthers to hang around the inner-city polls to intimidate and harass voters. This is not about race as much as this is about how Obama did not win most States, Obama only won most large Cities of which is where most of the violence occurs while Obama's only answer is to try and take away the U.S. Second Amendment that ensures the separation of powers, then give guns to only a police-state while most people in the rural parts of the Country will not let the Government take away their right to bear arms.

I recently noticed a bumper sticker on a truck in a rural part stating "bullets might get expensive and you might not get a warning shot" only a fatal shot. The most embarrassing of news publications in the last year, whether printed or televised, is how nearly every news publication from three months before the election up to the day of the election, had Hillary Clinton winning the election by at least 5 percentage points. I believe the Democrats and their corresponding media so desperately wanted to remain in power that the media mostly checked large inner-city polling stations while banishing the rest. If landowners do not get a larger percentage of the vote then their rights must be secured to prevent the infringement of their rights.

Universities use the Greek philosophy of separation and reunite with fraternities and sororities, however, the issue is that the Colleges discriminated and did not respect the same effect from separation and reunite of father and daughter. The issue with many Colleges is they teach without potency then manipulate the dictionary with urban slang from mostly single students when that is what the spurious imposters, frauds and fakes did when concocting the New Testament.

Exhibit A: inner-city strip clubs.

Exhibit B: playboy models.

Exhibit C: Hollywood.

Exhibit D: Divorce.

Where is the highest divorce rate per capita? Hollywood, California.

Rather than perverts intruding and debauching when only opposing father and daughter closeness, others would have appreciated similar merit from my sons without discriminating if the closeness was with my prior wife Angeline rather than my daughter. Others irony and discrimination caused my lawsuit when after every sired child was merited, regardless of whom I was closer, I could have immediately counter attacked and immediately killed others, however, popular public opinion would have continued to make sleazy excuses to belatedly discount the potency, health, and merit of every sired child while neglecting their encroachments.

I must restate, when every sired child was merited under my custody then there are no mistakes before others interpolated, interposed and degenerated that caused the mistakes.

I believe it is important for me to inform about another father and daughter relationship that are like most father and daughter relationships while father and youngest daughter's relationship would have been similar to the foregoing relationship if my youngest daughter's mother did not afflict a depression on her during the 2001 two week summer visitation that led me to send my youngest daughter to a private psychologist while I spent more time with my youngest daughter.

Conversely, her mother asked me for another week of
summer visitation that I granted the next year not
knowing that she was going to again afflict depression
the next summer while negligent of improvements. The
more typical father and daughter relationship was with
my eldest daughter while that relationship was about
directing her towards scholastic studies while having
my wife spend most of the time with my eldest daughter
to help my eldest daughter become more lady like.
When my eldest daughter had behavioral issues I
directed her to the Church and Bible study. The issue is
my eldest daughter still has some resentment towards
me for not spending more time with her. What my
youngest daughter is ungrateful for is not appreciating
the time I spent with her when I was giving her the
latitude to express herself and make more family
related decisions than many teenagers as long as she
was discreet to prevent others jealousy and invidious

discrimination that neglect overwhelming outward merit arising from my residence, direction and guidance.

I am not only angry that her mother depressed her before and after closeness, that trashy bitch insisted I spend more time with her and then conspired with unscrupulous cavaliers to interpolate and interpose using a political majority of fatherless debauchers to take what was my merited sons and almost destroy the respectable profession that I had diligently worked on for more than a decade. None of the intruders that encroached deserve forgiveness.

Personally, psychoanalytically, and religiously it is burdensome when compelled to exclusively consider medicine, law, and theology while others only waste time when only philosophically considering the foregoing entities without sired considerations, superior computations and supreme calculations that was prudently cautious of belated intruders with their predatory and discriminatory encroachments.

When considering my second best friend (James) father's (Daniel) adulteress wife whom happens to be the biological mother of James while his mother fraudulently embezzled money from James's father's business to give to her boyfriend, and while James would be inheriting Daniel's business, then James's mother robbed not only father, she robbed son to give money to her boyfriend. The saddest day experienced during that time started as a happy day for those that attended, although, ended in tragedy and sadness for the attendees. The day was Daniel's 25th Wedding Anniversary and many gathered at his shop to celebrate while there was even a 25th Wedding Anniversary cake on the table, then Daniel walked in the shop looking depressed, and then the attendees asked around why, and were told that a week earlier

Daniel had discovered that his wife of nearly 25 years had fraudulently embezzled money from the business while the money was being used for things like a new car for her boyfriend.

The salacious, careless, and unscrupulous games of popular public modern opinion would belatedly state that James's mother's boyfriend won and Daniel lost when thinking that winning the girl won the game while there is no support from other women when thinking something must have been wrong with Daniel for his wife to cheat on Daniel when Daniel never cheated and was only putting in extra hours at his small business for his family. Getting more or less attention should not lead to adultery, especially when running a small businesses that usually requires wearing multiple hats and working extra hours.

As for Daniel's wife's boyfriend, he should have respected the husband of the wife before he manipulated her into adultery.

The foregoing story has some parallels after the poor conquered their opponents while selfishly and fraudulently slandering on the public record for political and personal gain, and then with no remorse, neither deserve further communications, although, my hope is that one day my writings will be traditionally passed down and my sons will learn from my writings.

Paraphrasing James Madison, the encroachments is what we must prevent when addressing private property that will separate and respect the free exercise of religion.

In 2017 I read how Ivanka Trump harmlessly displayed on twitter the letters and drawings she received from children that appreciated her efforts.

What happened next were twitter responses from jealous perverts that tried to imply those letters and drawings were from her father. First, because of her father those perverts will not get within 10 feet of her before being stopped by the Secret Service. Second, no matter what Ivanka does there are always going to be critics that criticize her and she must expect the criticism after taking an active role in the White House. The most perverted critics are those that shame the body when they are not related nor her boyfriend nor her husband, and might as well get a blow up doll or a cadaver if only interested in her body.

While most fathers prudently shelter their children from the perverted critics, after their mother pushed my youngest daughter into public scrutiny, she must either ignore the critics or counterattack the critics.

Ungratefully attacking progeny is the mistake my youngest daughter made because not only will her father put her back in her place, she will have to counter the critics, and her brothers that will inevitably remember that after living in the same house with father and daughter, my sons will inevitably realize there was less contention than most relationships before others interpolated and interposed with perverted speculation. Her brothers will inevitably get angry at her after they realize their future would have been brighter had it not been for her betrayal. As much as I tried to save sired daughters and sons, since I sired sons, then if I was impelled to choose between daughters or sons then let there be no doubt I will save sired sons first as I did in the first physical custody change that was mutually agreed upon from father and mother. My youngest daughter only became part of the physical custody change after she ran away from her mother and then called me from a pay phone on the inner-city streets of Baltimore, Maryland.

What I did not expect nor appreciate is my daughter's vicissitudes after being belatedly coerced with popular public modern opinion that interpolated, interposed and proselytized into the military industrial complex and an ecclesiastical New Testament with illegitimate, fraudulent and spurious imposters.

I already knew the popular public majority cannot scientifically compute the numbers while most cannot comprehend the intellectual words, therefore, the foregoing is the prudent reason for being discreet before "Democracy comes into being, after the poor conquer their opponents, slaughtering some and banishing the rest." The spurious imposters and belated swindlers only play confidence games that I will dismiss. Even if competing against the most notorious and violent sport, come on man, did you ask her father for her hand in marriage or did you salaciously plunder without compassionately considering companionship?

To hear some extracurricular departments, coaches and broadcasters tell it, there are no moral victories while recruiting people from inner-city street gangs whom hold a gun to another's head, plunder another's earnings and think they won while the person whom was robbed had previously hoped the perpetrator had the morals and honorable sense of ethical conduct.

Count not the vote, consider those that suffered while respecting the count of life, liberty and happiness. :-)

After I already redeemed my youngest daughter then after others brainwashed and coerced my youngest daughter whom already helped decipher the absolute conclusion while implying that others need not despair when there is more than a five million women surplus to choose from, then others have no valid objection.

In the aftermath, the dilemma has been whom should I kill under the U.S. Second Amendment after "a well regulated Militia, being necessary to the security of a free State", my virgin daughter whom experienced true love and then was brainwashed and coerced into slandering her father by her mother whom did not experience true love after molested decades earlier by her step-father? My sons that I saved first and then they ungratefully slandered their father? How about their mother's boyfriend whom years earlier attempted to take my sons while trying to void trade, and then disregarded the Maryland District, Circuit, and State Supreme Court orders then grabbed my sons and ran out of the public Courthouse? How about the Director of the socialistic welfare-state of the Iredell County North Carolina Department of Social Services that strip mined and only supports mothers that embezzle from fathers? How about the fraudulent social psychologist whom was getting paid by I.C.N.C.D.S.S. then only believed in slanderous statements while refusing to believe truthful statements from their father, and then in malpractice refused to review the irrefutable evidence presented from their father supporting the truth, then negligently misdiagnosed their father, and then stated what he thought could damage their father to gain political favor for his political profiteering and personal financial gain. How about the assistant District Attorney of North Carolina whom is cavalier when thinking that mothers whom turn family members against one another do no wrong, and then without a victim charge fathers while gambling when trying to play popular public odds? How about vulgar commoners with Democracy that "only repeat what their rulers are pleased to tell them" while listening to sleazy vulgar trash and urban slang, then politically vote to ostracize and subjugate fathers after fathers favor sired gender balances and merited functional families against census gender imbalances and unmerited dysfunction?

When a race upholds a race and then when others object and state racism, are others on the verge of carrying out genocide? When considering a sired lineage and merited functional family, the Jewish religion and tradition, others discriminatory and anti-Semitic political persecution with sleazy vulgar trash, the unrestrained graffiti maliciously intends to harm.

What if I prudently knew, like most men, that the best tact was being discreet? What if most men knew the foregoing and dismissed my civil lawsuit because they did not want to publicly admit that they encroached and betrayed not only a legitimate father, they encroached and betrayed their fellow man while thinking I would not counter the oppression and challenge their ostracizing and totalitarian terrorism, then publish this Amendment.

What if I could not publish this book? What if before I appended Amendment I to this book, a female editor at a publishing company refused to publish this book because she implied Federal judges are the superior and supreme beings and do no wrong while I should accept their rulings without protest? What if she stated it was acceptable for their mother and her boyfriend to invade my privacy, and if after their invasions of privacy I published their before, during, and after actions then I was unacceptably invading their privacy? What if third parties used slander against me while using technology to invade my privacy to support their encroachments? What if there were no self-publishing companies that would publish my real and intelligible words my way?

In the 1996 case of the Unabomber whom bombed people associated with Universities, Ted Kaczynski, also known as the Unabomber, was a child prodigy and entered Harvard College at the age of 16. While at Harvard, a psychology professor made Ted a research subject for ethically questionable human engineering experiments on Ted of which Ted eventually rejected.

Ted earned his bachelor's degree from Harvard in 1962, then his master's and doctorate in mathematics from the University of Michigan in 1966 and 1967, and then became an assistant professor at the University of California, Berkeley, although, abruptly resigned two years later. In 1971, Ted moved to a remote cabin in Lincoln, Montana. In 1978, Ted began his bombing campaign. While I do not condone Ted's fatal bombing campaign before he published his manifesto regarding the erosion of human freedom and dignity, what I can understand is that during the prime of his life there were not many publishers that would publish and market his works, therefore, he bombed for the purpose of leverage to compel national publications to publish his works of which after he outwitted the F.B.I. he was published on the front page of the Washington Post. If I could not publish my words my way through a self-publishing company, I might have considered the way of Ted Kaczynski, however, now that I can publish my words my way then like after Ted's publication, him nor I have any intent on bombing others. I also understand the Government tracked my movements in case they thought I decided the time is now for vigilante justice.

As my technical profession attests, I advocate technology for home and business, especially for security rather than hackers using technology for fraud or political blackmail. I also do not crave national attention with politics thereof, therefore, a publication without marketing is acceptable since I would rather stand on my written words and eventual readers, and then word of mouth for the eventual policy reforms.

I believe most of this book has been a collaborative effort, although, being enslaved to write a book after others belatedly intruded is not something I want another to have to live through.

From a lawyer's perspective, time is money while I believe I earned more than the 13 million dollars requested in my civil lawsuit from time served. I also believe others have fraudulently deprived a tranquil future and then forced me to work overtime for the next 13 years to make up for the last 13 years that others wasted. There are many men that would have killed for less when if I knew 13 years ago that others would waste the next 13 years, then like I stated on the back cover of this book, I would have immediately killed the belated intruders. If every homeowner maintained their right to bear arms on their private property, then their rights would not be infringed from ostracizing in the Constitution, of which is the real intent of the U.S. Second Amendment of which makes the Democracy in the Constitution think twice rather than only once if Democracy had all the guns and formed totalitarianism from tyranny of the majority.

Is the occasion an Anniversary or Birthday? Is the occasion Christmas or Thanksgiving? Is the occasion Halloween or Independence Day? Is it trick or treat?

A trick is wearing makeup and dressing out as someone else then acting out. A treat is being yourself.

After a skilled man whom can support himself and his family experiences true love and the natural beauty of his woman, and then when she goes out and wears makeup, his first question is why is she wearing makeup when she goes out? His second question is she wearing makeup because her friends wear makeup and she is trying to be like everyone else rather than her natural self? His third question is she working for a business and wearing makeup for more attention to trick men into more business? His fourth question is she wearing makeup because she craves attention that she is not getting at home? His fifth question is she trying to attract other men into a relationship with her?

The problem is that a man might only ask himself one or two of the foregoing questions and not think deep enough to find more answers.

Either way the results are distrust that causes more distrust while the foregoing is one of the reasons why a man prefers his woman as a homemaker while men work with men without women causing distrust outside the home and in the workplace. The foregoing is why many did not appreciate the merit from my daughters before they interpolated, interposed and degenerated.

The merited value was for first, the environment had been corrupted with single mothers from dysfunctional families that could not support self nor children while relying on adultery and a socialistic welfare-state to embezzle from fathers. Second, since daughters were older than sons, my daughters could help tutor my sons, then perhaps later contribute as a respectable school teacher to help other children in the future.

The belated New Testament attempts to stand on an unscientific and impossible conception with a step-father and spurious son Jesus advocating that his disciples covet thy neighbor then forgive the trespasses while washing the feet of a prostitute. It is too bad the spurious words of the New Testament have been mixed into dictionary definitions while debunking thereof has taken several years of study. Many men in the Old Testament Jewish religion, Muslim religion, Romans, scientists, and individual men such as Shakespeare oppose the dogma of the priestly cross that believe in a spurious imposter. The U.S. Supreme Court is only upholding areas and privacy of woman and man while letting step-fathers in rather than privacy from siring and merited children. The poor that follow thereof might now only repeat what the unscrupulous cavaliers and their pussy whipped rulers are pleased to tell them. Before the New Testament, there is Genesis with Adam and

Eve, then Genesis Chapter 19, then Moses mitigating with the 10 Commandments. In 2007, after others invaded my privacy, encroached and electronically sieged my private property with propaganda, then after I told a firefighter no one is inside, I walked away from my house fire with the intent of never returning to the City of Statesville. The City representatives attempted to entertain the extrajudicial prejudice of mob-rule with their inexperienced or uneducated vacillating opinions, and then without a victim, compelled years of Court appearances in servitude to a City that invaded my privacy. I did not enlist nor ran for public office. I am a private citizen whom believes I do not owe any City, State, or Nation anything other than a share of taxes for sharing public property. I am not going to spend the rest of my life in public servitude, therefore, walking away now is with the same intent of never returning to a City that caused personal injury and substantial grief.

What a man does not need is a trashy bitch asking him to spend more time with her while she seduces his senses and then later conspires with unscrupulous cavaliers to rip him off with an unmerited, insensible, immoral, unsentimental and insensitive siege. Rather than walking away, the alternative perspective is an armed revolution when a man enlists the aid of his fellow man. The cause is securing liberty for a man in a way that does not take liberty away from another man of which must consider a census gender count.

There were five competing religious sects during the debate of the Bill of Rights. Religious liberty is secured when separating the public establishment of a religion against diversity of religions without encroaching on another's private property. The judiciary is responsible for ensuring separations. If a judiciary neglects rights then a judge might grant a warrant to have barbarous goons infringe on religious liberty and encroach on private property without being held accountable. The enlisting cause then results in members of the Army reorganizing such as when Army Veteran Timothy McVeigh aided the cause of his fellow Army service member Randy Weaver against a negligent judiciary.

An impotent mother fucker and sons of a bitch want to play games with only votes while there is no game when there is a sired gender balance and merited functional family against a census gender imbalance and unmerited dysfunction. The ostentatious and belated critics want to run off at the mouth and then after summoned in Civil Court they do not show up. There is either agreement or agreeing to disagree until death do we part. I could have immediately killed the belated intruders, although, whom other than potent experience could have written the absolute defense?

After a father and every sired child is merited, then his son after siring becomes father and every sired child is merited, and the alternative is considered, there is a mother with a fatherless dead son overdosing on the inner-city streets then daughter becomes mother and brainwashes sired children into slandering their father. The worse influence is a television station neglecting separation while advocating a negligent mother and is why I threw a four pound hammer at the television.

Throughout my life I usually walked away from an inner-city trashy bitch because I knew the unskilled government was rigged and prefer to use lobbyists with extortion for taxes and socialistic welfare-states with weak mothers to embezzle and swindle fathers. It has only been in the last few decades that a government has resorted to swindling and embezzlement. It is mostly Democrats that advocate socialistic welfare-states using the Department of Social Services.

When I grew up in a suburb of the U.S. Capitol from mostly biological fathers as heads of households that respected the diversity of religions and privacy thereof, the only time I seen the police is when the police were buying doughnuts at the convenience store while I did not hear of Social Services with their socialistic welfare-state until visiting larger corrupt Cities, of which I usually walked away from throughout my life.

I believe in family, friends, genuine love and affection, not ruining thereof with malicious acts by a third party alienating affection while compelling to compete with public servitude and ostentatious critics. While there are many people that supported me in one way or another during my writings, unfortunately many were hit and that is what happens when people invade another's privacy and want to play politics. After I was in the middle of two States, Maryland and North Carolina, that were stating the contentious conflict was like a civil war, and since I did not want another to be compelled to live through intrusive politics while discriminating against another in the future, and saving the beliefs and efforts of my sired and merited children when in my trust and custody, I believed writing and publishing this book was and is my responsibility. While there were some enjoying moments while writing this book, there were some emotions that I preferred not to have to relive, not only regarding my family, regarding empathy and sympathy for another family such as the Weaver family. There were many more days reliving the legitimate and rightful indignation after others unmerited, insensible, immoral, unsentimental and insensitive siege.

Neither Democrats nor Republicans have all the answers and while others tried to place me in the middle of either party, and in doing so, both parties were hit in one way or the other, therefore, securing privacy is the best tact in the future until the people directly involved are amicably and amiably ready for publication and can civilly share nice thoughts.

AMENDMENT II

The fundamental foundation of the judicial system is if 'B', whether an individual, group, or political entity, encroaches on 'A's private property then 'A' can either immediately bear arms, or 'A' can rightfully call the police for support of 'A' while the police can then bear arms on 'A's behalf, of which I believe is the safest way, plan and purpose of the U.S. Second Amendment. The foregoing restraint can prevent tyranny, whether from an individual or tyranny of the majority, before depriving the rights of 'A' then belatedly and arbitrarily wasting the time of 'A' to either ostentatiously profiteer and salaciously entertain belated intruders, or to politically intercept intimate and intellectual properties to compile demographic statistical voting data while discriminating and using offensive smear campaigns against another party to remain in power, or take over another party.

After I introduce exhibit 'A' in Court and get the opposition on the stand, then no one will get passed "Daddy" in the first line drawn on the last day in her father's custody. At this point the case is won without having to include signatures from sired sons or merit thereof when I will and can debate either or. Others risked their father summoning others in Court, or their father immediately executing another, or attaching explosives to the department of socialistic, socialized, superfluous, superficial and frivolous waste of time.

I do not believe justice is 3 1/2 years of wrongful incarceration without my day at the counsel table. I state from a State's Supreme Court that without Rights an unmerited Democracy is injustice.

Do not ask why the opposed did not subscribe to the socialistic welfare policies of the socialistic welfare-state if next time others are not so lucky, and another is immediately killed, or explosives kill their advocates.

Most modern American majority relationships are imperfect. What if an unrestrained individual or unrestrained majority encroached and then tried to arbitrarily use what the majority was ostentatiously and salaciously trained into what might be a perfect relationship and then criticize and repress a couple without the majority experiencing a perfect relationship?

What if after a repress there were some premature lapses in judgment of which after invasions of privacy led to antagonism and debauching? What if the end result before others encroached and invaded privacy was absolute perfection? ☺

What if others only wanted to play word games without considering census gender counts while there was a five million women surplus, and then I decided rather than play frivolous games I released her from her obligation and then considered the five million women surplus and dating a woman whom only wanted to seriously and sincerely consider one man for herself?

What if years later after reminiscing was considered the couple in question overcame others oppression and then recommunicated, like the email I received on the day I filed for a default judgment in U.S. Civil Court?

The absolute intent was my responsibility for a merited future for my sired children while maintaining the mental health of my children when considering reminiscence for my children if there were any lonely times in their future. The foregoing is my preference for positive thinking rather than negatively repressive and depressive thoughts.

When in my custody my children overwhelmingly experienced more positive thoughts than negative thoughts before others invaded privacy, repressed underwhelming negative thoughts then stepped over them without considering their merited achievements and bright future. We should never let anyone outside our reminiscence depress the more merited and pleasant thoughts of our reminiscence.

The issue with intrusive Democratic voters with their perverts strip mining my second daughter and then taking my sons is I absolutely and unilaterally object from a sired gender balance and merited functional family. While intrusive Democratic voters state anything against Democratic voters is a con, I state man up from a sired gender balance and merited functional family.

The problem with the intrusive Democrats is they debauch then thieve from the merited to support the underdeveloped, unmerited and poor with the unrestrained. I recall there was a time when my children were underdeveloped, unmerited and poor, and then after I gracefully developed them they became merited and successful.

In so far as others libelous, unmerited and inferior smear campaigns against a sired gender balance and merited functional family, the intrusive intruders went to the extent of trying to use neighbors, remote satellites, eavesdropping and wiretapping when regardless of their ostentatious show, they will not find harassment from me against any woman when I can prove I was politically persecuted, harassed and pursued to cause to suffer because of belief in such a way as to injure.

More than a decade ago I pondered the general census gender imbalance and unmerited dysfunction against a sired gender balance and merited functional family, and decided others extraneous interference and excessive entanglement is political persecution.

I then researched the U.S. Supreme Court decisions substantiating the same, and then years later discovered others belated and unmerited denial.

Their mother then regressed them back into the underdeveloped and unmerited poor when relying on Democrats to debauch them while trying to make me feel sorry for them and pay their mother whom regressed them and led them into a debauching rather than my children earning and supporting themselves from what they learned from their father.

Moreover, while a sired gender balance and merited functional family can balance the budget, a balanced budget Amendment suggested in years past from Republicans can avoid a Government shutdown while Democrats have no right to shutdown Government.

As for the modern President Donald Trump and his controversial tweets, while I mostly agree with his 2017 State of the Union Address, I only agree with the first 20 minutes of his 2018 State of the Union Address.

After a non-politician became cajoled by partisan politics for a year, after the first 20 minutes of his speech he became too political, as if he thought he was the father of another father's sired children of which is the gravest mistake of his Presidency.

While there were times I agreed with the President after 20 minutes of the 2018 State of the Union speech, there is a chamber for debate after 20 minutes.

I resent an impotent and inexperienced judge forcing me to meet with a social psychologist to take a test of which in return reported back inconclusive results while leaving the social psychologist to either professionally consider the merited evidence presented from their father, or unprofessionally discriminate and neglect the merit then side with a libelous and politically offensive smear campaign with unmerited malpractice.

I state whom needs a political social psychologist digressing into socialistic statistics with the socialistic party of WWII Germany when trying to force adults into testing, and then when there is inconclusive data returned, side with a libelous and politically offensive smear campaign with unmerited malpractice against not only a father, a father whom is a merited professional and the one writing the code that processes the data and whom already computed the successful results.

As it turns out the coder others tested has a test harness referenced in a URL in this coder's U.S. Civil Court filing referencing multiple Presidents and every U.S. Supreme Court Justice at the time of filing. What if I was already the King of the Country, and then a fatherless politician overturned the balance? I would then reconvene the Nuremberg trials of 1946 then hang their appointed judge, then tell the social psychologist "off with your head" while attendees state "dilly, dilly".

APPENDEX VII

According to a documentary titled "CIA Secret Experiments", in the concentration camps during WWII the Germans were not only incinerating the Jewish, the Germans were using mind control experiments on the Jewish. In the wake of WWII, from one Democracy to another Democracy, the U.S. Government was engaged in a large number of secret experiments while exposing unknowing members of the public to biological and chemical agents, and attempting to develop brainwashing techniques with mind control. The U.S. Government was covertly developing lethal bacteria, the plague, anthrax, brucellosis, poisons, etc ... More than once the CIA simulated an attack on a City in America to evaluate how easy it is to poison a City by releasing bacteria in a subway system then monitoring samples throughout the subway system. In a matter of minutes the entire subway system was infected.

After WWII, America entered into a tripartite agreement with Canada and Great Britain. Britain's research into biochemical warfare is carried out at an Army base in southwest England. On any given day there was at least one American researcher at the facility. In May 1953, Britain was developing what was at that time the most lethal nerve agent known, Sarin. The experiments were conducted on military volunteers, although, the service men were only told they were helping to find a cure for the common cold. Six Air Force men were led into a sealed room, given a respirator and told to roll up their sleeve. They were then given 20 drops of a clear liquid on their arms. The liquid was Sarin nerve agent. The men started sweating with difficulty breathing. After 30 minutes they were released outside while gasping for air. Two days later, another group of six were led into a sealed room, then after more drops were given, they began foaming at the mouth and died in less than an hour. The corresponding paperwork stated the purpose of the experiment was to determine the lethal dose of Sarin. It is believed that a 43 year old American man named Frank Olson, a biological weapons researcher for the Army, and whom also worked for the CIA researching germ warfare, witnessed the deaths. Frank Olson told a colleague that he seen things he thought should not be going on, of which led the U.S. Government to conjecture and start having doubts about whether Olson could be trusted with top secret research.

At the time, the U.S. Government thought LSD could be used for mind control and were experimenting on mostly minorities with LSD because the CIA did not put as much value on the life of the minority as the life of people in the majority. As a reward for participating, the minorities were given heroin. The U.S. Government was also covertly hiring prostitutes to lure men in rooms to slip them drugs in the attempt to get men to talk while the U.S. Government recorded their conversations. The drug LSD was also given to people in Germany of which was witnessed by Frank Olson whom again became disturbed and again told a colleague. The colleague told the CIA and the CIA thought Frank Olson could be a serious problem if he told anyone outside the Government of the covert CIA experiments.

Frank Olson and six colleagues attended a clandestine meeting on November 18th, 1953. They were joined by members of the CIA. According to CIA documents, Frank Olson and most of his colleagues were slipped LSD in the attempt to see what people in the group would say. Later in the meeting the people in the group were told they were given LSD. A CIA consultant later wrote a memo stating the meeting was designed to trap Frank Olson. When Olson returned home he was somber and upset. Olson told family members he wanted to quit his job. Instead of the Amy and CIA accepting his resignation, they sent him to New York for psychiatric counseling, of which was not really psychiatric counseling, since the person he talked to in New York was an Allergist.

In a Manhattan hotel room on Thanksgiving weekend in 1953, Frank Olson plunges to his death from the 10th floor. Another person, a CIA agent, was in the 10th floor room. The CIA told the Olson family his death was from suicide. According to the medical report, Olson's neck and face were badly lacerated. At the funeral the casket remained closed while the explanation was he was too badly injured to be seen.

On June 11, 1975 the Washington Post reports the CIA broke the law. The report states a civilian employee of the Army unwittingly took LSD then jumped 10 floors from a Manhattan hotel window to his death. No names were given, although, Olson's son knew they were talking about his father. The Olson

family went public while the major networks attended.

The source of the Washington Post article was the

Rockefeller Commission Report triggered by Watergate

and is a Presidential inquiry into elicit domestic

activities by the CIA. The Olson family decided to sue

the CIA for their father's wrongful death. The Olson

family received $750,000 for Frank Olson's death, and

President Gerald Ford apologized to the family.

Spurred by media reports, Congress launched an

investigation while stating the CIA had a disregard for

human life. Representatives of the CIA testified while

the Director of the CIA stated he had directed others in

1973 to destroy all documents related to mind control

experiments. Some documents were not destroyed.

Frank Olson's son Eric was not convinced his

father died from suicide. Eric exhumed his father's

body. A professor whom examined the body stated

there were no lacerations evident on his face and head of which contradicts the medical report at the time of Frank Olson's death. A large bruise was found above his left eye of which was not in the medical report at the time of his death while the injury did not result from the fall since Frank Olson landed feet first then backward. During Eric's investigation he discovered the same year Frank Olson died the CIA published the agency's first assassination manual. In general terms, the manual stated the ideal way to murder someone and make it look like an accident was a fall from a window of at least 75 feet high while the victim should be stunned with a blow to the temple above one of the eyes before dropping the victim. The professor whom examined the body stated the description in the manual was identical to the bone bruise found on Frank Olson's head. The professor believes Frank Olson was deliberately and with malice of forethought thrown out the window.

The report from Congress stated there were 80 institutions contracted by the CIA for mind control research, including 12 Hospitals and 44 Universities.

Regarding the Washington Post articles, the Washington Post was being delivered near Ted Kaczynski's cabin. Perhaps Ted read the articles before starting his bombing campaign while writing a manifesto against Universities using mind control research, of which was conducted on Ted at Harvard University.

What about trust, what about love, and what about the happy ever after? ☺ What we do not need is brainwashing into reneging, slandering, and defaulting for the purpose of entertaining vulgar commoners with intrusively belated pandering and stories of deception.

Whom would have thought after a 21 page religious writing in 2005 followed by wrongful incarceration there would be 422 numbered pages 13 years later?